42 Rules for Divorcing with Children

Doing It with Dignity & Grace
While Raising Happy, Healthy,
Well-Adjusted Children

By Melinda Roberts
Foreword by Heather Armstrong

E-mail: info@superstarpress.com
20660 Stevens Creek Blvd., Suite 210
Cupertino, CA 95014

Published by Super Star Press™, a Happy About® imprint
20660 Stevens Creek Blvd., Suite 210, Cupertino, CA 95014
http://42rules.com

First Printing: September 2012
Paperback ISBN: : 978-1-60773-072-9 (1-60773-072-3)
eBook ISBN: 978-1-60773-073-6 (1-60773-073-1)
Place of Publication: Silicon Valley, California, USA
Library of Congress Number: 2012947212

Trademarks

All terms mentioned in this book that are known to be trademarks or service marks have been appropriately capitalized. Happy About®, nor any of its imprints, cannot attest to the accuracy of this information. Use of a term in this book should not be regarded as affecting the validity of any trademark or service mark.

Warning and Disclaimer

Every effort has been made to make this book as complete and as accurate as possible. The information provided is on an "as is" basis. The author(s), publisher, and its agents assume no responsibility for errors or omissions nor assume liability or responsibility to any person or entity with respect to any loss or damages arising from the use of information contained herein.

Praise For This Book!

"What I wish my parents had known when they got divorced (twice.)"
Casey Mullins (http://mooshinindy.com)

"In her compulsively readable book, Mindy Roberts deconstructs the myth that couples with children can truly get divorced. With humor and insight, Mindy explains why remaining a family after divorce is crucial for the well-being of the children, and provides practical tips for reconfiguring post-divorce families. Every divorcing couple, or any couple contemplating divorce, should read this book."
Virginia Gilbert, MA, MFT, Specializing in High-Conflict Divorce, and HuffPost Divorce Blogger
(http://www.virginiagilbertmft.com)

"In *42 Rules for Divorcing with Children*, the author, Melinda Roberts, addresses some of the most significant issues divorcing parents face. Her rules are offered with compassion and understanding along with real-world advice that can be immediately put to use. This is a smart guide that I recommend to any parents who want to avoid the heartbreaking mistakes too often made when divorce divides a family!"
Rosalind Sedacca, Founder, Child-Centered Divorce Network
(http://www.childcentereddivorce.com)

"Mindy Roberts's book is a must read for anyone with children who is in the initial stages of a separation, currently separated, or divorced, or even those who are engaged in high-conflict co-parenting. Mindy's take on what to expect and how to realistically manage these situations by keeping your eyes on the prize—happy, healthy, adjusted children—will help keep you sane and smiling. The marker of success is not how we handle things when they are working, it's how we handle things when they fall apart. You are not alone, and keeping this handy book beside you will help you find the success you're looking for—no matter how hopeless you might think things may be!"
Diane Holcombe, RN, Life and Wellness Coach
Supporting You Through Transitions
(http://www.clarifyyou.com)

"If you don't think you need *42 Rules for Divorcing with Children*, you're dead wrong. If you're not getting a divorce, your best friend, coworker, sibling, or even your mom will be, and they'll need the 42 Rules to help them through it successfully. So go out, buy half a dozen copies of Mindy's book, and hand your divorcing friends and relatives *42 Rules for Divorcing with Children* along with your sympathies and the phone number of a good divorce lawyer."
Anne-Marie Nichols, publisher of *This Mama Cooks! On a Diet* (http://www.thismamacooks.com/)

"Mindy Roberts's *42 Rules for Divorcing with Children* is an honest and thoughtful book on a difficult and painful topic. It's chock full of humor and insightful advice on how to divorce with dignity and grace, while doing the best by your children to build a better life going forward for the family that was and is to come.

Mindy's advice and information are also helpful for family members who are on the sidelines of those going through the process and those evaluating their current relationships.

What especially resonated with me was the repeating message to release resentment and move forward with empathy and hope. To me, that acknowledges all the seething mess of bad feelings and encourages channeling it into refocusing on the life you want to live forward."
Jeanne-Marie Jasko

Epigraph

"When you tell your kids you're getting divorced, hand them cupcakes first."
Daphne Roberts, Age Ten

Dedication

These rules are dedicated to my children above all, whose willingness to let me into their worlds helps to keep mine centered, safe, and loving.

I also thank my husband, Steven, who taught me as much about divorcing with dignity as my own mother did, and that's saying something.

To my mother, my rock: my appreciation and gratitude are always implicit, and can never be expressed often enough!

Special thanks to my ex-husband, Gil for being the father of my children and for always, always being there and loving them to infinity plus one. He is their OP.

Acknowledgments

As names in this book have been changed to protect, well, everyone, I'm unable to thank most of the people whose input I valued. Fortunately, not naming names is handy in the event that I might have forgotten to mention someone very, very important. Therefore, please assume that it is YOU I'm thanking: for your support, contributions, trust, selflessness, humor in the face of disaster, and epic divorce stories.

Leaving out my mother is career-limiting at best and dangerous at worst. So I hereby acknowledge that I could not have written this book without the help of my mother, Patricia Lorimer Lundberg, PhD, Professor of English and Women's Studies; CEO, poet and editor; and the best role model a young, terrified, divorced mom could have. Thanks, Mom: You've taught your (and my) children well.

Contents

Foreword by Heather Armstrong

I was ten years old when my mother and father told me and my siblings that they were getting divorced. We sat around the kitchen table, and I remember the sound of my legs squeaking against the yellow vinyl of the dining chair when I took my place. I thought that if I could crawl up inside that noise, then I wouldn't be able to hear what I knew they were about to tell me, news that had been years in the making.

Those years were miserable for everyone in our home. My brother and I used to hide in the dark of my room on the far side of my bed and listen to my parents yell at each other. Eventually those arguments became so scary that my sister, my brother, and I sought refuge outside the home. My sister turned to her boyfriend while my brother and I turned to our best friends.

Christy was my next-door neighbor, and I shared her twin bed during sleepovers that happened almost every night of the week, even during the school year. Sometimes we'd play in her backyard before her parents fed me dinner, and we'd hear my own parents yelling in their bedroom about fifty feet away. Christy and I never spoke of it. In fact, she'd always tug me inside when she saw me stop to try to make out what they were saying.

Whenever I did sleep at home, I'd find my mother in tears every morning, a zombie, a vacant shell. I'd watch her wash her face in the bathroom sink and beg her to tell me what was wrong.

"Nothing," she'd answer, always. Not once did she elaborate.

But I knew better, kids always do, and so I decided that I was going to fix things. If I made good grades, she'd be happy. If I excelled at everything I tried, she'd be happy. If I vacuumed the house in perfect lines, she'd be happy. And if my mother could just be happy, then the fighting would stop. Surely this would work.

I was the child who took my parents' divorce the hardest. Yes, I was the youngest, and my brother and sister could process that split with more maturity than I could. But the truth is that I thought I had failed everyone. I had tried to fix it, and it broke anyway. All that furious work I had done, and the family still fell apart.

I wish my parents had had this book when they were going through all that pain. I wish my father had stopped himself from turning to me, from rocking me back and forth in his lap and asking in my ear why my mother wouldn't come back to him.

I like to think that I learned from my parents' mistakes, because it's been over eight months since I separated from my children's father, and not once have they witnessed an argument. That's not something to brag about, no. I mean, it should be this way by default, right? But now that I'm going through this pain myself I can forgive my parents more than just a little bit. Emotions run high and wild. When my idea of fair gets trampled on or the resentment boils and overflows, it's hard to resist screaming at a wall IN FRONT OF EVERYONE.

I have not been perfect during this time, not even close, but before we decided to separate we made it clear to each other that the kids would always come first. Because of what I had gone through when I was ten, I had a working blueprint. We'd honor their routine and their feelings and their confusion. We'd communicate with them often and openly, never speaking ill of each other. They'd never have to ask us repeatedly what was wrong, and neither of us would whisper one word into their ears about our own pain. They'd never have to seek refuge with someone else because being around us was too unbearable.

Foreword

I feel very lucky that I have this book while I'm right in the middle of everything, because while I know many of the mistakes to avoid because of my own parents, there was a lot I was surprised to learn. I reread the sections on finances, resentment, and grief multiple times. Also, I am terrible when it comes to asking for help, and this is the most overwhelming situation I've ever been in. I have walked right up to the brink of an emotional breakdown once or twice in the last few months, and it's nice to be reminded of the reasons why I can and should step away for a while.

Also, when the homework and assignments start flying like gunfire, I will wear out the pages that detail how to transfer children between houses (I've already dog-eared that section).

This book helped me fill in many of the blanks, and I know I will reference it often in the coming months. If you have found yourself wondering how on earth to honor your children during this gut-wrenching time, or if you have no idea where to start, consider this your blueprint. Turn to these rules when you are feeling weak. Most importantly, let it help you feel a little less alone.

HEATHER ARMSTRONG
http://www.dooce.com/

Heather Armstrong, a former Web designer, started publishing dooce(r) in early 2001. Heather has won numerous awards for her work on dooce.com including Best American Blog, Best Designed Blog, Best Writing for a Blog, and Weblog of the Year, and in 2008, she received a Lifetime Achievement award. In addition, Heather was named #8 in Forbes's "The Web Celeb 25" in 2008 and 2009. Heather has been profiled in The Wall Street Journal, The New York Times, The Washington Post, USA Today, Forbes, and Businessweek, amongst others. Heather has appeared on ABC's Nightline, NPR, PBS, ABC World News Tonight, and NBC's The Today Show. The blog dooce is one of the most widely read personal sites on the Internet and has a passionately loyal following. She is the author of the bestselling book It Sucked and Then I Cried: How I Had a Baby, a Breakdown, and a Much Needed Margarita.

Divorcing with Dignity and Grace

In 2004, my husband and I decided to get a divorce after eleven years of marriage, years that gave us hope; heartbreak; and three beautiful, happy children.

There's no easy way to divorce with children; you have to learn by doing. You can start by putting their confused, fragile hearts and minds first, and doing your best to build a new life for all of you without destroying one another in the process. You don't have to like your ex (or "OP" as we shall be calling the Other Parent in this book*).However, you must try, for the sake of the children, to treat the OP exactly how you hope the OP will treat you. This is critical for your children to have any chance for a future that includes a loving, healthy, adult relationship of their own. Your children have not fully individuated yet, and they can't help feeling that if either parent is perceived as bad, then *part of them must be bad.* They will internalize whatever you project toward the OP, so project your best side.

Now that my own children are seven-year divorce veterans, I asked them what advice they'd give to other parents, hoping that they would tell me what went right and what went wrong in our own experience. My four-teen-year-old son shrugged. In response, my eleven-year-old son said, "My advice is that parents shouldn't ask their kids to do their writing for them." My ten-year-old daughter said, "When you tell your kids you're getting divorced, hand them cupcakes first."

Our children have repeatedly told the OP and me how much they appreciate the way we've handled things. They like that we try to get along and that we all get together often, celebrating birthdays and holidays together. If we can't do the whole day, they try to wake up at one house and sleep at the other. We both promised that we would never, ever love them less or hate the other parent, because how could you hate the only other person who loves them as much as you do? (My condolences to those who are living another reality; I totally get it, and my heart goes out to you. It takes two to tango, and some people can't even find the dance floor.)

Granted, our shared life in divorce is possible because we live in the same county, we like each other a lot more now that we're no longer married, and we both want the children to have as intact a family experience as possible given the circumstances. Unfortunately, this is not possible for a lot of folks.

Try to have a divorce characterized by dignity and grace, at least with regards to the children. In seclusion, feel free to practice your archery with the OP's photograph. I don't care what you do to get that anger out; just don't let the kids witness it. They didn't ask for this, and they cannot begin to fathom what comes next.

You can make it easier on yourself and on them. Come on, I'll give you 42 rules to follow.

*For purposes of clarity, I'll define a few terms for this book. The chances of everyone having the same players and relationships are slim and emaciated, so I'll be as broad and inclusive as possible (hint: this a recurring theme).

OP: Other Parent. I've tried and discarded ex or DH (short for "dear husband"[1]). The Other Parent may not yet be an ex or especially dear at the moment, so we'll go with the undisputable and maximally neutral "Other Parent." So, OP it is.

Children/Kids: I'm not fond of using an acronym for children for this book. We are talking about children collectively. In short, I will use the terms "children" and "kids."

---

1. http://www.urbandictionary.com/define.php?term=dh

Part I
Making the Decision—You and the OP (Other Parent)

Making the decision to divorce is one of the most difficult and painful things you will ever do as a parent. Getting to the place where the decision is *unanimous* while agreeing on how to proceed is a close second. Coming in third is figuring out how to deconstruct your life and put it back together again. Doing all three things well is the ultimate hat trick. Hopefully, this section will help you give it your best shot.

- Rule 1: Rules Are Meant to Be Broken
- Rule 2: Curb Your Resentment
- Rule 3: Do These Four Things First!
- Rule 4: Begin How You Mean to Continue
- Rule 5: Take the High Road, but for God's Sake, Don't Take Out a Billboard Ad
- Rule 6: Look at Divorce as a Journey, Not an Outcome
- Rule 7: Choose a Mediator Together

When two people decide to get a divorce, it isn't a sign that they "don't understand" one another, but a sign that they have, at last, begun to.
—Helen Rowland, *A Guide to Men*

1 Rules Are Meant to Be Broken

I don't want you to think that my perspective is some Pollyanna bullpucky; it isn't.

Not everyone will come away transformed by this book. I have seen and heard about some very good and some horrifically bad divorces and have made an almost unconscious—certainly in-formal—study of them. Over the last six or seven years, friends, families, and complete strangers have expressed astonishment at what my OP and I are willing to do to make our divorce work *for* us rather than *against* us. We set a credible example of what can be accomplished if both parents are willing to cooperate and put their kids' interests ahead of their own.

We have advanced degrees in holding our noses. Our tongues are calloused and blistered from the biting. Our faces hurt from the strained smiling. But we have also managed to share so much more than just our allotted percentage of our children's lives, and seeing the genuine love and devotion we each have for our children has softened our attitudes and strengthened our resolve to keep it up.

Not that we want to live together, of course. Let's not get carried away. I don't want you to think that my perspective is some Pollyanna bullpucky; it isn't. We've worked damn hard to divorce with dignity and grace. I know that for some, cooper-ation and civility just aren't possible, especially when one party is obstinately determined to make the divorce a personal vendetta. When that happens, a little piece of your soul is lost, and that certainly changes your perspective on things.

It is possible—not easy, but possible—to tear down walls of resentment and, together, reevaluate and reorient your divorce process so that the emotional, physical, and financial well being of the family is driven by what the children need. They are not pets, or accessories; they are what we are either gifting to or inflicting upon the world as our legacy. Children emulate what they see growing up, and if there is any chance of changing that for the better by putting aside your own bitterness, resentment, and revenge impulse, there is a chance to short-circuit the legacy of divorce.

In short, depending on what you absorb and take away from *42 Rules for Divorcing with Children*, you may be able to save your children some of the heartbreak you are experiencing now or have already experienced. Resentment is self-defeating and debilitating and just about the last character trait you want to instill in your children.

This book has only one goal in mind: to help divorcing (or already divorced) parents minimize the damage of divorce and maximize growing conditions for your new life with your children and the OP. It's your story to write. You don't have to act out anyone else's play; there is no currency in doing things just because it's the way it's always been done. The status quo is not its own justification. Dare to flaunt a social convention by being more inclusive, more tolerant, "fairer," and more focused on children than people expect from a divorced couple.

Depending on how you integrate the advice in this book—and not just my advice, advice from a lot of people who have been through much worse—your mileage may vary.

2 Curb Your Resentment

Resentment is corrosive, debilitating, and completely counter-productive.

Resentment is like taking poison and waiting for the other person to die.
—Malachy McCourt

Malachy McCourt was spot-on. Resentment is corrosive, debilitating, and completely counter-productive.

Everyone is entitled to wallow, as that is between you and your conscience, and perhaps anyone who chooses to be around you while you do it. Wallow away. Everyone needs to indulge those feelings, acknowledge them, heal, and move on. You can always circle back; in fact, I recommend that you do, and that you bring ice cream and movies.

Resentment is completely different. Resentment is something that you think is between you and another person, something you think is felt by that person through sheer force of will and la-ser-focused rage. The truth is, they aren't partic-ipants. They can't feel it, may not be aware of it, would not attach the same value to it as you do, and might even dismiss it entirely. You wear re-sentment like you wear your skin: it is subjective, intensely personal, always there, and always vul-nerable and sensitive, and others haven't the faintest clue how you feel encased in it.

Shed it. Get help! Don't feed your resentment; rather, try to learn how to let it go.

You have a long road ahead, one that disap-pears into the horizon, circles the globe, and is right there behind you when you look over your shoulder. If you do this right, you will be walking this road indefinitely, and you'll want to travel light. Do you really want to give piggyback rides to real or imagined slights, indignation, and your own personal life-disaster gag reel on permanent loop? No one else is watching it, and you are giving rent-free space in your brain to someone from whom you've already decided to separate.

Worse, that person is dragging around his or her own blooper reel of things that he or she may regret or resent, so the person isn't even suffering along with you. You are suffering in parallel. I bet you never considered that. It's because resentment is intensely personal and cannot be forced upon another in any meaningful way. You can't (and shouldn't) expect anyone else to feel and see and think as you do, so any energy you spend on resentment is wasted on the OP and bad for your own well being.

I don't pretend to know the best way to shed resentment; I find myself tipping over into it periodically, but it happens less frequently as time goes by and acceptance sets in. With that comes a feeling of freedom, and—wait for it—hope! You no longer have to factor that other person into your formula for personal fulfillment. Anything you do from now on is a product of your ability and willingness to let go, look ahead, and realize that you will never have power over how another person thinks or behaves. In fact, what another person thinks is none of your concern or business! Remember the golden rule about treating others the way you'd like to be treated, NO MATTER WHAT. That applies even if you are 100 percent right and the OP is 300 percent wrong.

You and you alone have power over your own thoughts and behavior, and you have an opportunity to start fresh with new habits that don't include spending any more time launching unhealthy thought missiles at an unappreciative and probably oblivious audience.

3 Do These Four Things First!

The divorce process is not linear, and neither is this book.

The divorce process is not linear, and neither is this book. (Seriously. It doesn't matter if you read it in one swoop or pick a rule at random. Have at it.) No one really knows where to begin once a couple has decided to divorce. It's awkward at best and paralyzing at worst. Try to piece things out and chunk this massive challenge into small tasks. Remember this old joke?

Q. How do you eat an elephant?

A. One bite at a time.

For starters, there are four things you and the OP can and should do immediately. To wit:

1. Agree on a plan for communication to the kids and to others. (More on this in the next two rules.) Get it in writing using a counselor or mediator; it will make things smoother and aid in the event of emotionally impaired recall.

2. If one of you moves out, immediately put a co-parenting plan in place that focuses on the children's well being. Include detailed plans for visitation, dropping off and picking up the children, medication/health management, activities management, and where to house all the children's stuff.

3. Establish a percentage split for all assets (50 percent in community property states), including cash (keep a list with approximate values).

4. File officially with the court to set a date of separation. It will protect you in ways you cannot yet imagine.

Please be sure to consult laws in your own area! In California and other community property states, earnings, debt, and property acquired after the court-filed date of separation are considered separate property. Secure your perimeter.

After the date of separation, you cannot share earnings, you cannot be held liable for the OP's debts, and you cannot indulge in revenge spending without it blowing up in your face. All debt you accrue from that date is yours and yours alone.

Correspondingly, all income earned after this date is separate and will be used along with historical data to determine support issues. You will probably have to establish a marital standard of living to settle support issues. The marital standard of living is a calculation of the joint earnings of the number of years you were together and is used to determine who will pay whom support, how much, and for how long. If there is a discrepancy between your income and the OP's income, the court will use a calculation (sometimes called The Dissomaster,[2] a standardized formula) to come up with the official numbers.

Because the process is numbers-based, there is nothing much you can do to affect the outcome (unless of course you come to a mutually agreeable settlement on your own). Be sure to disclose EVERYTHING. I'm serious. This is no time to get petty. It's harder than you think to hide assets from a competent lawyer, and you do not want to wind up in court because you gave false or incomplete information. It will only cost you money and pay for your attorney's second home.

An example to avoid: A couple with small children divorced in California. She was a stay-at-home mom; he was an executive. Through mediation, they quickly and cooperatively settled division of assets, custody, and future child-rearing policies, but they could not agree on temporary spousal support. He made an offer, she wanted more. He offered a big bonus to avoid a court fight. They stalemated. It took two years and nearly $100,000 in legal expenses to build cases for each side. In the end, they settled privately for less than the original offer the morning of the court date. By not cooperating, they bankrupted the children's college funds, decimated the marital assets, and both lost.

Don't let the lawyers be the only ones who win.

---

2. http://www.cflr.com/products/dissomaster.php

4 Begin How You Mean to Continue

Life is messy. We can't be everywhere and see everyone at once. It's a constant pulling apart and coming back together.

The habits you form now will soon become routine. Establish good ones that are sustainable. Choose to embrace change going forward. The only thing in this world you have control over is how you react to your environment. It may seem easier to begin one way, thinking that you'll change as you feel more comfortable later, but it really doesn't work that way. It's harder to invite people or traditions back in once you've tossed them out.

By many standards, my OP and I have engineered an enviable post-divorce existence. We are friendly, go to our kids' events together, celebrate holidays together if we are in town, and make sure the other parent has a cake and homemade cards coming from the kids on birthdays. We share extras like tuition and medical care, and we are good about tracking who paid what when and how to balance that out. Neither of us is rolling in dough at the moment, and empathy for the other's financial hardship runs high. We may not agree with why there is hardship in each household, but we both know you can't get blood from a stone, and beating it only gives you a sore fist.

We both have excellent relationships with the kids. We are both crazy in love with them. When we split, we agreed that I would buy the house from him so the children would continue to live in their birth home with all of their things and still attend their schools for minimal disruption. We have never refused one another time with the kids and accede to whatever special occasions warrant a change in the routine.

Throughout our divorce, we've emphasized the family unit as something immutable, something permanent and indestructible. Moms and dads may divorce, they may split one unhappy household into two happier households, but they will never NOT be a family. And, especially in our case, parents really can be a better team in two houses.

For starters, neither of us wanted to miss 50 percent of the children's lives going forward. That meant we needed to share time, information, and respect for the children's psychological well-being. We even share stories. The children especially cherish any shared memories you can give them. Take it from someone who's been there: it's awful to have only mom memories and dad memories.

There's no way to separate physical custody from emotional attachment, or legal guardianship from caring and concern about the daily lives of your children. We love our children equally and have arranged our lives for optimal unity. We communicate, we fill each other in; we encourage the children to stay in touch with the other parent when they are with us, and we are co-conspirators for surprises and Christmas wishes.

I understand that empathy is close to impossible when you can't even have a civil conversation, but hear me out: those kids only have two parents, and they are depending on you to help them navigate new waters. Think about this: the OP is probably the only other person on the planet who loves those kids as much as you do.

Life is messy. We can't be everywhere and see everyone at once. It's a constant pulling apart and coming back together. The nuclear family is a myth. The reality is so much richer.

5 Take the High Road, but for God's Sake, Don't Take Out a Billboard Ad

"I'm taking such a high road where you are concerned, I'm having lunch with God."

A friend showed me a text from her OP that read, "I'm taking such a high road where you are concerned, I'm having lunch with God." Those aren't the words of someone taking the high road. Those are the words of someone missing the point. If you have to defend your words and actions as being high-minded, you're already tripping over yourself. If you truly take the high road and act in the best interests of the children and others involved, your behavior will need no self-defense.

Taking the high road means letting go of things you cannot control (like how clean the OP will keep the house and what the kids are allowed to eat) and doing everything you can to ease this transition after divorce and set a good example for your children to follow.

Avoid expressing negative opinions of the OP, especially in front of your children. They already know you have issues; they will lose respect for you if you can't keep a lid on it. Children are perceptive, and over time they will come to know what's right and what isn't. I flat guarantee you: badmouthing the OP will backfire on you.

For the record, I'm not very good at this at times. I've had to put this book down for weeks at a time because I struggled with breaking the same rules I was laying down for others. BUT! I try hard enough that my children know my heart is in the right place; I am human and fallible but also determined to do what's right.

If your divorce was precipitated by infidelity, physical or emotional abuse, or substance abuse, this is part of the story you do not need to broadcast. In general, people's inability to empathize in a helpful way is directly proportional to the level of discomfort your confession causes in the other person. For these kinds of issues, find a trusted confidant who knows something about abusive or other extreme situations; ideally, this would be a therapist or some other counselor who will treat you with respect and keep your confidences. Your friends might listen with rapt attention and ask for more details, but it COULD be, in SOME cases, for the drama. It could also be because they have no idea how to react. For someone who hasn't been in that situation, it's nearly impossible to imagine how it really feels.

Beware: the need to understand and the shock of discovering uncomfortable truths will likely prompt these friends to share your story either to get another's perspective or in a misguided attempt to rally support. Look: if you'd wanted the world to know all about it, you'd have taken out an ad! Burdening others with information they cannot understand or process will prompt them to seek understanding in ways that may blowup in your face. AND, it may get back to the OP AND piss the OP off, AND then you've basically emptied a canister of Aqua Net into an already fiery mess. That's a great visual, isn't it? Don't try it; I will deny all implication that I suggested such horrifying (but awesome) actions.

In the meantime, keep your dignity. DO NOT fall into the trap of thinking that drinking or drugs or affairs or the need to control and intimidate were more important to the OP than you were. The OP did not choose them over you. The OP lost you because of them. That person made bad choices, and not having you for a spouse is the consequence. Be strong, hang in there, and remember you are NOT alone. Taking the high road rewards you with an abundance of dignity and grace.

6 Look at Divorce as a Journey, Not an Outcome

"Mine the darkness and see by the path you leave behind."
—Andy Young

I left this rule sitting like an orphan for a long time, circling back and skipping over it many times. What do I know about the journey? I'm only seven years, five months, and nineteen days into it as I write these words, counting from the day my OP and I agreed that we would in all probability not continue our marriage. Who am I to draw anyone a road map?

Where's MY road map? I didn't—I mean, I don't—have one. I have a ring inscribed with the words: "Mine the darkness and see by the path you leave behind." It is my talisman for touching base when I don't know what the hell to do. It reminds me that sometimes there is no illumination to light my way through the tunnels, let alone to light any passable way for you to follow. Perhaps you should light your own way. Maybe the light will fill up behind you as you mine the darkness, and maybe it will light the way for those who come after you. But it needs to become your own personal path that you take. And maybe you will be wrong, but if you are, here's hoping you learn something from it, as I have.

So, I only have my own winding pathway to show you. I think it's a good one, and the view is pretty nice, there aren't too many bumps, and it's lit and passable, for the most part.

Divorce for you is going to be scary and unpredictable at times. All you can hope for is the clarity of vision to make good choices, the wisdom to see how your actions have led to where you are, and companions to sometimes hold the lamp and take second watch.

Oh, I sound like I'm full of shit. Here is some real advice, what we'll call the Nine Tenets of Instant Therapy, Right on the Chin. Sort of like my mother's joke about instant therapy: slap, slap, snap out of it.

- Decide that you are going to move forward and not spend time, money, or energy being angry about the past. If it's over, it's over. Move on.
- Stop wasting anger and bitterness on things that will never be the same ever again; let it go. It's not easy, and it hurts like hell until you put it down and give it some time.
- Make the most of your children's future and yours too. Help them carve new tunnels and light their pathways.
- Make yourself a life. You may never have your old life back, but you can have a better one.
- Lead by example. Be the change you want. Clichés persevere for a reason; you are depriving yourself of a teachable moment if you discount them completely.
- Repair your damaged tunnels to the future. You may feel damaged. You most likely are, and your children may feel that way too. That is part of divorce, so repair what you can, discard what you can't, and let time do the rest, forging a way forward.
- Love each other hard. As they say, people may never remember what you said, but they will forever remember how you made them feel.
- Understand that you will heal. Someone close to me once said, "Wow. This is really, really painful. I must be learning something." Learn to recognize that feeling for what it is and leverage it as best you can.
- Ask for help if you need it (and you do).

7 Choose a Mediator Together

Mediation fosters success, not surrender.

Mediators are trained to make sure each side is fairly represented, heard, and understood. Mediation is cheaper than taking it to court, more civil, and less likely to cause you to later suffer divorce remorse. (I made that up. You're welcome.)

The mediation process is about healing quicker and creating a safe outcome for the children. Going to mediation is a smart move if you want to avoid an expensive, lengthy, and probably ugly court case. Above all, you need to watch out for your own interests as well as protect whatever assets you can for yourself and your children.

Repeat after me: Mediation promotes success. It does not spell surrender.

There is an excellent article by Lynette Khal-fani-Cox called Getting Divorced or Separated? 7 Financial Mistakes Not to Make.[3] In it, Cox exposes faulty assumptions and poor decision-making. I especially liked the author's comments on mediation:

> Retaining a divorce mediator or arbitrator is one way to accomplish a less combative divorce. A mediator is an impartial divorce specialist who works to help couples reach an "equitable" divorce settlement.

---

3. *Getting Divorced or Separated? 7 Financial Mistakes Not to Make* by Lynette Khalfani-Cox.

But be warned: Hiring a mediator just for the sake of "impartiality" or in an attempt to "keep the peace" is usually a bad financial move—a really bad one—particularly if you assume that a mediator will look out for your best interests.

"The primary goal of the mediator is to get a settlement. And any settlement means the mediator has done his or her job," says Susan Carlisle, a Los Angeles area CPA who specializes in family law. "Although the best mediators do their [best] to get the settlement as equitable as possible, it's your job to negotiate well for what you need and want. The mediator can't do that for you."

That's why the best mediators always recommend that each party in a divorce also have their own consulting attorney."

Here is the short version of the seven financial mistakes Khalfani-Cox lists. I wish I'd had this list while going through my divorce.

1. Thinking that a mediator will protect your financial interests;
2. Hiring the "best" lawyer that money can buy;
3. Keeping joint credit cards and loans;
4. Insisting on hanging on to the family home;
5. Trying to maintain the exact same lifestyle;
6. Having a weak property settlement agreement; and
7. Failing to change your will and insurance policies.

Remind yourself that mediation can be speedier than the courts, unless you perversely wish to prolong the process, for which you will pay. While you need to trust your mediator to fashion an equitable result, you also need to protect your interests. Mediation professionals exist in abundance because there is an abundance of money to be made in divorce—you will have your pick. YOU are paying them, so do your part to speed up the process.

My epiphany about the appropriate level of personal investment that a legal professional should have in a case came when a friend thanked an attorney profusely for good advice and a prompt response, etc. The attorney stopped her midsentence and replied, "When you get paid, I get paid." He was as motivated to get the file off his desk as she was to have the case resolved. Closing a file is pretty much all the closure a legal professional needs. You might need a bit more closure, but get done as quickly as possible with the mediation part.

Part II
Internal Communication between You, the OP, and the Children

Consistency has helped your children feel safe and secure all their lives, and you are about to introduce a massive change. How you and the OP facilitate that change will determine not only how well they adapt this time, but how they will respond to change in the future. They must be able to trust both the source of the change and their own ability to survive it.

- Rule 8: Decide How, When, and Where to Break the News
- Rule 9: Never Tell the Children Why You Divorced
- Rule 10: Be Available to Talk with the Children about the Divorce
- Rule 11: Live Nearby
- Rule 12: Work from Big to Small, but Don't Ignore the Small
- Rule 13: Arrange Things from the Children's Point of View
- Rule 14: The Rest of Your Life Will Always Include the OP, If You're Doing It Well

I realized it wasn't divorce that's devastating; it's the way divorce is handled.
—Blogger Molly Monet

8 Decide How, When, and Where to Break the News

Emphasize that you will be a better team in two houses.

We told our children during snuggle time in bed, when everyone was feeling safe and close. We didn't want a formal, nerve-wracking meeting where everyone sat with hands folded in laps. Fortunately, we had slowly prepared, after the OP found a job and another place; he had been a stay-at-home dad for four years, so we waited to break the news until he could support a separate household.

The kids were upset: the eldest (7) inconsolable, the middle child (4 ½) quiet, the youngest (3) not really getting it. We emphasized that we would always be a family but that they would spend part of each week at mom's, part at dad's.

We were lucky that we could cooperate about how to break the news, focusing on the love, in a safe space. Not everyone will have that luxury. If you have any control over how, when, and where you tell the children, choose to do it lovingly, and—if possible—with dignity and a united front. Practice if you can, because it will be awkward as all get-out and—bet you dollars to donuts—one of you will blurt out something inappropriate. The most important thing perhaps is that you both show love during the conversation. Hold your nose if you have to; this is not about you.

- Plan ahead. Agree on what to say and not to say. It's not helpful for one parent to say it's temporary and the other to say it's perma-nent.

- Emphasize that it's because of discord between the parents, NOT because of anything the children did, said, felt, or dreamed. Let them know that together you considered every possible alternative. Do not dive into the swamp of real reasons.
- The children will argue. Given the choice between a happy parent in another household or an unhappy one under the same roof, nine times out of ten they will prefer you crying in the next room. This is not about giving them what they want, but about what will enable the family to function better. The kids will suggest that you just go to your rooms and later hug and apologize and decide together what channel to watch, like they have to do.
- Emphasize that you will be a better team apart. Sometimes it's just not possible for two people to live together and be happy, or safe, or kind. Giving each parent some space away from constant friction will help everyone to act better towards one another. You can't be irritated at the state of the house if you are the only one running it.
- Listen to the children. The decision isn't open for discussion, but feelings, fears, and logistics are. It will take time to get through their concerns; don't cut the talk short.
- If possible, touch each other while talking. This was important to our kids. They wanted to keep touching both of us, and years later they still try to draw us into group hugs. Put aside your aversion and give this small gift to your children. Soon enough they will have only separate memories with each of you.

Everyone will suffer. I have only heard of one instance where the children said, "Well, we wondered how long it would take you to realize you shouldn't be married." Chances are that your children won't be that perceptive or have that perspective. Go easy on yourselves; there is no painless way to do this. Everyone will cry.

But! You can take comfort that a better life is coming. You'll develop your own ways to pay bills, fold the laundry, park the car, load the dishwasher, and clean the bathroom. This is not trivial stuff; it's amazing how free and hopeful you can feel about making these choices alone. Knowing you can keep the doors closed in summer and fold your shirts in thirds instead of halves—man, it's the bomb.

9 Never Tell the Children Why You Divorced

Kids really don't want to know why, no matter how old they are.

I know; I sound crazy. You cannot get through a divorce without confiding in someone! Talk to your parents, family, friends, counselor, priest, or rabbi. Do not talk about it to your children. Monumental mistake, and not fair to your kids.

Why not tell them the truth? Here are several excellent reasons:

1. Your truth will differ from the OP's truth.
2. Your truth will differ from the actual truth.
3. There is no actual version of the truth.
4. There is no truth that can be reconciled with the above.
5. They do not want to hear any of it.

If you tell the children something other than what you've negotiated with your co-parent, they will forever have tremendous difficulty reconciling competing "truths" and so will distrust all of them. Deep down, most children think they could have done something—anything—to make things turn out differently. They will agonize over their own actions, their own sense of self. You do not want to burden them with something beyond their understanding. Believe me, I've been there.

I am a child of divorce and a divorced parent. I can't tell you how many years it takes to get over it, because I'm still not at peace. It took twenty years for me to stop wishing my own parents were back together. Sure, I knew on an intellectual level that they were better parents and people for splitting. At the gut level? My inner child never stopped wanting to undo the thing that made it impossible to ever be with one parent without missing the other.

Even your adult children will not want to know the gory details. I still thank my parents for not telling us, and I credit them with my own decision to allow my children to remain innocent of any knowledge that will corrode trust in their parents.

When I told my mother I was writing this rule, she fired off an email that stunned me. In it, she talks about how her own mother gave her way too much information:

> One day my mother told me she was divorcing my father. Then in my late thirties, even knowing intellectually that all marriages go through peaks and troughs, I did not want to hear this. Parents aren't supposed to divorce after going through the joy and hell of more than thirty or forty years together. I didn't want to know why. She told me why. I was devastated. Having been divorced myself at 30 and at the time progressing through my own complicated years of life divorced with kids, I did not want to know why. My parents didn't divorce, but I never got over knowing why they might have. Why did she tell me? I was busily not telling my own kids why their father and I separated for a year before divorcing, though during that year I fully expected to get back together. [Author's note: You what? Wanted to get back together? Argh! Curse you for telling me!] Divorce became inevitable, and not all that dignified. I tried very hard not to tell the kids why. Kids really don't want to know why, no matter how old they are.

I'm still sitting here at my keyboard, wondering why the hell she just told me that. I didn't want to know that they might have gotten back together! It's easier to absorb now, thirty years later, but still! I wonder, how could it have worked? What would life have been like if I'd been able to see my father more than every other holiday and six weeks during the summer? Good grief, I need a drink to get past that one. Let's move on to the next rule.

10 Be Available to Talk with the Children about the Divorce

They didn't ask for this. If you can't give them the information and reassurance they need, get them to someone who can.

As I said in Rule 9, agree, if you can, never to tell the children exactly why you divorced. It all comes down to an inability to live together peacefully, and in a way that provided a healthy environment for the kids. The kids DO NOT want to hear bad things about the OP. If you think you're scoring points for your side by taking shots at the other, you are sadly mistaken. Undermining love and trust in the OP will backfire, and regaining that trust will take far more effort than it did to undermine it.

The A-Number-One priority for talking with the children about the divorce is to concentrate on how it will affect THEM. This is not the time to talk about yourselves. It's not about you at the moment. It's about helping them sort out their thoughts, feelings, fears, and logistical questions.

I once attended a speech by Frank Luntz. Mr. Luntz, then a leading Republican strategist and pollster, and architect of Newt Gingrich's "Contract With America" in 1994, spoke about what he considers crucial to controlling and winning policy debates. (Which is what divorce negotiations feel like, am I right?)

I had a real "WOW" moment during his speech that had nothing to do with politics—and he was as surprised as I was when I told him about my moment and how I was planning to use it. Here's the gist. He'd outlined a very basic strategy for communicating effectively: if you want to explain a plan, a concept, or a change to an audience, you have to use the 50/20/30 rule. You spend 50 percent of your time explaining the "Why," 20 percent on the "Therefore," and 30 percent on the "How." I liked that fully half of it is the setup. Too often, we dive in with the headline, the change, and everyone is too busy chewing on that to hear the "Why." And I like that the "Therefore" is brief in comparison. No sense getting stuck there. Move along and get to the How so we can all relax. I really liked what this guy said, so I felt so bad about approaching him afterward.

I told him about my "WOW" moment, and said that I was going to use that rule in an important communication, and soon. He perked up.

"We are going to have to tell our children next week that we are divorcing, and I think that this kind of structure will really help us with the message." His shoulders sagged.

"Oh, don't tell me that." He paused. "How old are they?"

"Six, four, and three."

He winced. He thought for a bit and said, "OK. After you tell them, stop. Stop talking. Let them ask questions."

I nodded. "That makes sense. As much as we need help with the message, we need help with the boundaries—when we're nervous we tend to talk too much and end up muddying the message. Thank you. I know this isn't the usual application, but I wanted to tell you that I think it's brilliant."

And you know what? It works. When you find yourself unsure of what to say, don't talk. Let them ask questions, and do your best to answer them in a way that shows you are considering things from their perspective.

11

Live Nearby

Your children will keep their emotional suitcases half-packed, waiting for you to come to your senses and get back together.

You may feel divorcing is absolutely necessary. Your children, however, will keep their emotional suitcases half-packed, waiting for you both to come to your senses and get back together. If you cannot give them togetherness, then please, please try to give them proximity.

When I was a child, my parents separated for a year and then divorced, and we moved two states away from our father. My brother and I, four and five years old, could not understand what was happening. I am sure they prepared us, but I don't remember any of that. I just remember leaving dad behind, waving, and him growing smaller as we wound down our long, gravel drive.

Mom and my brother and I moved to Chicago, where she was born and raised. We moved into her old neighborhood, went to her grade school, and attended mass at the church where my parents were married. So having familiar people around gave us a sense of security. Mom knew where to live and how to arrange day care while she worked. Though we had a joint custody arrangement, we stayed with her during the school year and visited our father for part of each summer, plus every other holiday.

I felt devastated knowing that we would probably never again be together with both our parents. There was Mom Time and Dad Time. Mom Memories and Dad Memories. Before Divorce Time and After Divorce Time. No Skype, no email, no cell phones, and no answering machines to record a parent's loving voice.

In short, it sucked ass. It was lonely. It was depressing. Friends and family surrounded us, but we could never shake that awful feeling of homesickness for the absent parent. We had friends at each home base, but they never met one another. It took a lot of emotional energy to prepare to leave one parent and to integrate into the OP's household, especially after our father remarried and started a second family, and our visits felt farther in between.

I tell you this story to give you a small taste of what it is like for a child to move far away from a parent. Fallout lasts for decades. If at all possible, live no more than a few miles apart. When I divorced, the OP rented a house one mile away. Even then it was heart-wrenching for our children to go from one home to the other. They knew they could pick up the phone or be driven to the other home whenever they needed reassurance, or a blanket or toy, or just to prove that the OP had not abandoned them forever. No exaggeration.

The OP and I now live fifteen miles apart and still share custody equally. We negotiate the drive between houses every couple of days. Both of us are willing to accommodate the kids' need for continuity in friends and activities. It consumes a lot of time, gas, and energy, not to mention sometimes annoying negotiating time, but they have learned that mom and dad are ALWAYS there. That doesn't stop them from wishing we were back together, but they have adapted quickly and well to separate but nearby households. They trust in us as parents to have their best interests at heart. They are grateful for our staying close by. It is worth everything to know that they have that measure of security.

12 Work from Big to Small, but Don't Ignore the Small

You also have to work out custody for the Easter Bunny and Santa Claus.

Take a deep breath. Your kids are scared and need you to help them make sense of how life will change in big and small ways, even if you can't make sense of it yourself.

Big Things for You:

- Housing. Where is everyone going to live? How much will it cost to run two households?
- Custody. Who will stay where and when?
- Schools. Will anything change?
- Transportation. Do you each have a vehicle that will carry all the children plus a parent? If you have a sports car, say goodbye.

Big Things for Your Children:

- Friends. Will I be able to have them over to each house? Will they still like me?
- Bedrooms. Will I have to share a room? Will I still be able to share a room? My kids each got their own room, but sometimes they are lonely, so we have a lot of sibling sleepovers.
- Toys and Games. Can we get a Wii for each house? A bike? Where will my baseball equipment live?
- Pets. Will Fido move around with us? No? Who will take care of him when we are gone and make sure he has his squeaky?
- Clothes and Stuff. If I forget something, will you ferry us back and forth until we get the hang of this new arrangement?

I don't even want to get into homework, a Big Thing for EVERYONE. In the six years since the OP and I divorced, we still struggle with this.

Textbooks are left under beds, reports started at one house don't get to the other house to finish, we bookmark websites on mom's computer but can't remember how to find them on dad's. We spend a lot of time scanning, emailing, and ferrying parts of books and papers between houses. Try asking teachers for a second textbook. It beats constantly hearing, "I left it at the other house, can I turn it in later?"

Very, Very Small Sampling of the Small Things:

- Shoes. What? You came here barefoot and don't have shoes to wear?
- Uniforms. Buy two of everything. Yes, it's expensive. So is anger management therapy.
- Cell Phones and Paraphernalia. Keeping track is maddening.
- Notices from School. ARGH. Weekly envelopes go home on Wednesdays. Guess who doesn't have custody on Wednesdays? Never knowing what is going on drives me up a wall.
- Teeth. If a child loses a tooth at one house but sleeps at the other, where does the Tooth Fairy leave that freaking dollar? You also have to work out custody for the Easter Bunny and Santa Claus.

Have "Mirror Houses" if you can. Anything you can do to ease the transition into two households will help the kids (and you!) cope. For instance, I went out and purchased the same sheets, comforters, quilts, pillows, and drapes. The OP bought the furniture, and I provided the familiarity. It looked familiar, felt familiar, and eventually smelled familiar. INVEST IN THE FAMILIAR!

It gets easier, and you will tap into powers of organization you never thought you possessed. You will learn to be an administrative team or go crazy. Separate the administrative bits of parenting from the interpersonal relationship you've had with your OP. You don't have to share a bed, but you have to share schedules. You don't have to talk about your feelings, but you have to talk about the children's needs, responsibilities, and feelings. It's easier to concentrate on issues concerning the children than on those you occasionally wade into between you and the OP. Repeat after me: you are a better team in two houses.

13 Arrange Things from the Children's Point of View

You childproofed your house for their safety and security; why should this be any less important?

Each child has his own toolkit of feelings, defenses, self-comforting ways, and ways to get comfort from others. They especially have their own ways of getting comfort from their parents—my kids approach me differently than they do their dad, and we approach them differently from each other—hell, we approach each CHILD differently. These differences were there even before you decided to divorce. I ask only that you make an effort to respect those differences.

In your new setup as a separate household, make an effort (to the extent possible; this is a book, not a wand) to provide the same kind of outlets, ways of seeking comfort, ways of having fun, and ways to keep communication flowing between you and your children, and between your children and the OP. Alienation is not allowed in your toolkit. Chuck that baby over your shoulder and move on.

If you can, involve them in the process of arranging your new life without giving too much over to them. It's scary, overwhelming, and not fair to overburden them, but give them just enough input so that they don't feel completely left out. Think team members, not assistant coaches (and certainly not owners).

> **Do:** "Oh, you want to have your bed on a different wall or your own private study space in the new place? Let's see how we can do that."

> **Don't:** "I have NO idea how we're going to make it. You kids have any ideas? Mommy's going to get a little drinkipoo and be right back."

Granted, not all the decisions you make will be in their favor, but they do need someone to take charge. Children crave structure, boundaries, and rules. Even silly rules work. In fact, I like to throw a dingbat into the mix just to keep them interested. ("No honking like a goose or I will put potty training photos of you on Facebook." "Anyone claiming not to have shoes will be sold.")

Try to make the major rules the same in both houses, including chores, discipline, etc. I see you looking at me like I'm crazy. I know there's no way to do that if you can't even speak to the OP let alone chart out behavioral goals; I said to try. I promise you this, though: I flat guarantee you that if they are forbidden to do something at one house and allowed to do it at the other, they will play you like a banjo. Eventually you will see the benefit of agreeing on a few things.

Now, there are different schools of thought regarding what to do when the kids break rules that have significant consequences, such as grounding or loss of screen time. Some parents want a consequence to be carried over to the OP's home if the duration is greater than the time remaining before they see the OP. Others believe it's not pragmatic to expect the OP to carry out a sentence you imposed. I personally believe that one should never assign a timeout one is not prepared to sit out, and that goes for toddlers on up to teenagers. "My house, my rules" means you don't get to say how things should be handled at anyone else's house.

While you're at it, try to have some consistency in routines such as meal times (good luck with that; I have never succeeded), bath times (or frequency for that matter), homework time, and play time. The worst that could happen is that the kids have to learn how to survive in each house according to that house's set of rules. The best that could happen is that there is a lot of consistency and overlap and transitions go smoothly.

After all, you childproofed your house for their safety and security; why should this be any less important?

14 The Rest of Your Life Will Always Include the OP, If You're Doing It Well

You will never not be a family, and no amount of wishing will make the OP go away.

No matter how painful the divorce, no amount of wishing will make the other person go away. You will never *not* be a family.

Have you ever been frustrated at having to share a computer with someone who does things differently? I have. The day I decided I would never share a computer again was one of the most liberating days of my life. (This was after a crash prompted my OP to reformat the disk before checking with me—I worked for the people who invented the damn computer; I was pretty sure I could get someone to shake the thing loose. I lost thousands of photos and personal files. But that's my journey.) My new Mac arrived, shiny, untouched. I set it up all by myself and never shared the password. It was safe. Impermeable. No one could hurt my new baby. I was starting fresh, knowing that anything that went wonky due to user error was MY error. I can't stand not knowing what happened to cause a problem, especially if I wasn't around when a whole lot of crap was installed on the machine. I'm a little passionate about my technology.

Look at the start of the rest of your life as rebooting a computer. You can start fresh. However, the programs, settings, and bugs you have introduced into your system remain. This is your chance to work on yourself. It is impossible to go through a divorce and not feel shame and guilt. Shame that you didn't keep your vows. Guilt over how your children's lives are changing. I don't care who started the process; everyone gets to carry the baggage.

Any shame and guilt you carry (the bugs) will cripple you if you don't deal with them. Ignoring these feelings will only prolong the pain and likely cause you to repeat mistakes or find yourself experiencing the same outcomes over an over. (Remember Einstein's quote: "The definition of insanity is doing the same thing over and over and expecting a different result.") Do something different (develop new features). Pick the ones YOU like, the ones that will make your life easier. You do not have to compromise on the little things anymore. No one else has your password.

I highly recommend listening to what Brené Brown (http://www.ted.com/speakers/brene_brown.html) has to say about vulnerability and shame. The two TED Talks I've watched and shared with others have reportedly *changed lives*. I've heard that her book is marvelous as well. Just give her a listen. Make the time. I guarantee you'll learn something about yourself. She goes into great detail about vulnerability and shame, and the necessary part they play for everyone. All her life, she pushed vulnerability and shame away, seeing them as weaknesses and something to be vanquished. She was astounded that they were critical to fully understanding her own actions and motives. It's really quite thought provoking.

The following is my favorite quote from one of her talks, which was more about her research than anything else, but I thought it applied to the process of divorce as well: "You gotta dance with the one that brung ya." You may not choose the OP today if you could do it again, but there was a time when you just couldn't imagine life any other way, with any other person. There was something good there once, and it's up to you to dig that up, dust it off, and use it in your new role as a divorcing parent.

Bottom line: children tend to fare better emotionally when both parents are involved and cooperate to minimize the lasting effects of divorce.

Part III
External Communication between You/OP/Children and Everyone Else

Here is where consistency is once again paramount. You and the OP must present a united front to the children, and your family as a whole will do best if you are able to present a united front to the world. If a united front is impossible, at least try not to contradict one another in an unproductive way.

- Rule 15: Agree on a Story and Elevator Pitch
- Rule 16: It Will Never Be Fair
- Rule 17: Make the Process Invisible to Others
- Rule 18: Decide How You Want Your Divorce Story to Be Told
- Rule 19: Can't Agree? Take a Timeout and Come Back Later
- Rule 20: Keep It Off Facebook!
- Rule 21: You Will Make Frenemies
- Rule 22: Get Therapy from a Therapist, Not Your Attorney—It's Cheaper

I'm not gonna say any more than I have to, if that.
—Chili Palmer, Get Shorty

15 Agree on a Story and Elevator Pitch

It's to everyone's benefit to have a matching story when word inevitably gets out about your divorce.

There are three stories of your divorce that you should have at the ready: one for the children, one for those close to you, and an elevator pitch for all others. (An elevator pitch is a pithy point made in the time it takes for a short elevator ride with a person. Be brief, be bright, and be gone.)

Sample story for the children:

Mommy and daddy have been fighting a lot, and we know it upsets you. It upsets us too, so much so that we have decided that the family will work better if mom and dad live in separate homes. It is not because of anything you did! It is the grownups that are having trouble getting along, and we think we will be a better team in two houses. We will still see each other; we will always be your mom and dad; and we will always, always love you, no matter what. We love you so much that we don't want to keep making the family unhappy because we can't get along. [If they ask why you can't just try harder to get along, ask them if they think they could get along with their siblings 24/7. That was an eye-opener for my own children!]

Sample story for family and close friends:

We've decided to divorce for reasons that may or may not be obvious to you. We've spoken with the children and reached an understanding between us. We are focused on working out the details ourselves in private in a way that we hope will minimize pain all around. The most important thing right now is for the children to feel safe, and to trust what we tell them. While we continue to sort things out, please love the children, spend time with them, and let them know they have safe places with you too. We would appreciate your not exacerbating their confusion by adding details, asking them probing questions, or offering well-meaning advice that may show either of us in a better or worse light. Please do not offer opinions or details they are not old enough to understand, or that might undermine how we are trying to conduct ourselves during this painful process.

Sample elevator pitch:

We've decided to divorce and hope to share custody of the children. For now, Parent A will be living here, and Parent B will be living there. It's a difficult time for all of us, and we've decided not to discuss the reasons for the divorce so that we can settle this privately and without harming the children. I hope you understand.

There will be those who won't be satisfied with these stories and those who will not be happy until you've shouted, HE/SHE IS A LYING SNAKE AND I CAN'T WAIT TO BE RID OF THAT SHITBAG! If you think it will short-circuit the painful conversation, by all means say it, but don't offer anything else. Psychologically, they are rooting either for or against you, and saying little enough will satisfy their need for drama without TMI.

Together, you need to agree on and stick to these communications. It's to everyone's benefit to have a matching story when word inevitably gets out about your divorce. DO NOT say anything beyond your agreed-on story to others that may get back to your children and hurt them. People will talk, and they may even approach the children with condolences in an effort to get more information. If they do not have the information, they cannot give it out. I cannot stress this enough!

16 It Will Never Be Fair

"Fair" doesn't exist as an objective measure.

You will never get fair in court, from your lawyer, or from friends and family. The OP is probably not inclined to offer fair to you. The cognitive dissonance involved will make it impossible to believe that something fair to you is also fair to the OP. It makes my head hurt just to think about it.

"Fair" doesn't exist as an objective measure. However, "acceptable" does exist for yourself, the OP, and your children. Don't expect a judge to suddenly see your side and make all the pain go away. (Chances are good that the OP is hoping for the same revelation.)

If you hurt the OP in pursuit of your version of "fair," you hurt your children by extension. Take it from someone well-versed in the practice of "acceptable." My new husband and I have six children between us, and we know only too well that "acceptable" is as close as you can get. (Although, when it comes to disputes over who gets more juice or a bigger slice of cake, here's the solution: let one child do the dividing, and another child choose which share to take. It's fascinating to watch the mental gymnastics involved.)

No one will ever win an argument by accusing you of being too nice, pleasant, flexible, or cooperative. In fact, don't even look for or think about fair. Think about and strive for acceptable given the here and now. Make your decisions, move on, and stop second-guessing yourself! Your kids will do plenty of that for you. What do you tell them when they complain, "It's not fair"? You say, "Whoever said life was fair?"

Yeah. Ouch. Hurts when that turns on you, doesn't it?

Nice in the long run will serve you and your children. They will model behavior they see, even if it is invisible to the naked eye, until one day several months down the road when you look at them and think, "By God! They've got it!"

Be a role model. Be the change you want to see in the world. Treat others as you want to be treated. Oh hell, just think of every corny thing you've ever told your kids when they were being unreasonable and recite them to yourself. IT'S NO DIFFERENT. This time, you are on the hot seat, and they are scrutinizing your every move to see how you treat the OP and are deciding how to treat you both. They are a lot sharper than you think, and will learn for themselves that the OP has warts without your help. That goes for you, too.

True story: A father had an unpleasant exchange with the OP in the process of picking up his children. When he got into the car, he apologized for their behavior, saying that it's never his goal to upset their mother or them. They immediately said, "Don't worry, Dad, we get it. Mom says stupid things sometimes. I love her, but man, does she say stupid things." He kept his hands at ten and two and stared straight at the road ahead, not sure whether to touch any of that. Finally, he asked if any of those things are about him. Their response? Yes, but they don't let her get away with it. "We get really mad at her when she says anything bad about you. We tell her not to talk about our dad like that." He was both proud and horrified.

Let them come to their own conclusions. They're smart cookies.

17 Make the Process Invisible to Others

People never tire of looking for juicy bits.

Remember, now that you are in the process of divorce you are automatically immersed in a fishbowl. Even if others don't have specific knowledge of your situation, and I hope they don't, they can sense it. This is the time to be very careful about how you speak to anyone about the OP or anything remotely related to the OP. This is a tough one, especially when the OP gives you so much ammunition.

A seemingly offhand comment can be colored so many ways it would make your head spin. Once, at the end of a party for our Little League team, I offered to help break down and load up the barbecue for whomever it belonged to. Someone looked at me and said, "Isn't it yours?"

Holy crap, it was! I didn't remember because we'd divvied up possessions six years earlier. And because I felt silly and had known these people for years, I laughed and said, "Well, it WAS, but I lost it in the divorce, you know."

Someone reported this "awkward moment" back to the OP at a game the next day. He defended me, saying, "You know Mindy has a wicked sense of humor, I'm sure she didn't mean anything by it." And he was right. And we both laughed about it later.

Now, in this community, our sons have been playing ball together from T-ball through the Majors in Little League, and all the parents know that my OP and I have a comparatively successful post-divorce relationship, yet the first offhand comment that could possibly be construed as negative still spreads like wildfire six years later. Jiminy. I carried that thing back to his house, dismantled it, and scrubbed out all the utensils for him since he was traveling the next day. That's the kind of relationship we have.

But people never tire of looking for juicy bits.

Everyday conversations take on a new weight, and they seem to continually circle back to the fact that you are divorcing. "I like your hair like that, it suits you," suddenly sounds like, "Good thing you did something different if you ever want to find another man." Learn to count slowly to yourself before responding or letting it light you up. I know, easy for me to say. But it is not easy to do.

Sometimes the best response is no response. If an ambiguous question borders on prying, follow Ann Landers's advice and respond, "Why do you want to know?"

Understand that this is true: there are more people than you can possibly know talking about your divorce, trying to dissect it, reporting clues back and forth, and trying to make sense of it. It's a gossipy game for some, a genuine effort to help for others. There is nothing you can do to stop it, but you can start growing a thick skin. You can't control what others say or do; you can only control your own actions and reactions.

You will be tested. I was sorely tested at a function when someone I've known twenty-five years said to me, "Don't worry, you'll find someone. You're still pretty." STILL PRETTY? It's moments like these that will really tighten up your chain mail. (Stay tuned for more about Frenemies in Rule 21.)

18

Decide How You Want Your Divorce Story to Be Told

Think very carefully about how you would like the collective memory to be shaped.

Your children will be telling the story of your divorce for decades to come. Think about how you want that story to be told. Children of divorce generally do heal. But we also remember.

My husband and I had dinner recently with my mom and stepdad. All four of us have been divorced. We shared stories. I realized all over again how important it is to think, as a parent, how you would like these collective memories to be shaped. Only later do we begin to see how we have shaped the stories around divorce and its afterlife.

That evening, my husband was surprised to hear the story of my father's remarriage, still a vivid and painful memory for me many years later. Just to clarify, we adored our stepmother, and to this day my brother and I think she is the kind of mother any child would be proud and grateful to have. We were thrilled for them, excited to see dad happy, and curious and interested to see a loving relationship (having never really seen one up close, at least that we remembered). There was absolutely nothing not to like about the fact of their marriage, but looking back, we might all have handled negotiations about the actual day differently.

Mom offered to drive my brother and me (we were eight and nine) across two states, stay in a hotel, and chauffeur us to the church and the reception (not intruding herself). Dad said no. There weren't going to be any children at the wedding. What do you mean, no children? We're his children. What if we just come for the ceremony? No. No children. We stayed home.

Looking back, I can intellectualize how they might have wanted to have that special day to themselves, but I think we've all realized that it may be best to err on the inclusive side. That is why, when I remarried earlier this year, all six of our children stood up with us. We couldn't imagine it any other way.

It wasn't completely anxiety-free. The kids weren't yet sure they wanted stepparents even though they approved of our respective choices and liked having more siblings. Right up until the day, there was a little edginess and fear of what others might think and how their lives would change forever. But you know what? We had an absolute blast. Looking back at the photos, I see the way each child looked at each of us, how they focused on us as we teared up during the vows or cracked up during the ring exchange. Somehow, those photos captured the mixture and evolution of everyone's feelings that day, and the predominant ones were of joy and happiness. Disclaimer: I'm not saying that with a shred of denial or overestimation. You can see for yourself in our online wedding slideshow (fabphotos.biz/MindySteven)! Pascale Wowak works in images and emotions like no other photographer I've met.

Try to be as inclusive as you can at family gatherings from the very beginning. Your children will thank you later. They will realize after the fact, perhaps long after the fact, that you were doing it for them. They need to know why you were or were not inclusive. Otherwise, they may make themselves crazy trying to supply their own rationale. If children don't understand something, they will self-supply explanations so that they can reconcile experience with resolution.

19 Can't Agree? Take a Timeout and Come Back Later

The goal isn't to prove who's right, but to reach an acceptable solution to a major disagreement.

The single hardest lesson for me to learn about coming to an agreement over seemingly impossible disagreements was learning how to disengage and take a timeout before the argument escalated beyond repair. As children grow, we try to teach them to stand their ground and to take defensible positions and above all not to bully or be bullied. What isn't as easy to teach—or to learn—is when to walk away from an argument in which you are probably right; possibly winning; and, at least from your perspective, certainly justified.

During a divorce, almost anything can become contentious, and when your blood is up, the OP is the last person to whom you want to lose or before whom you want to seem weak. That is why it is absolutely essential to disengage yourself when the argument has jumped the tracks, and set a time to come back to the table once tempers have cooled. Some call this running away; I call it doing everyone a favor by shutting up before you say something that can't be unsaid.

So, how do you know when it's time to back off? I have a simple yardstick: as soon as the subject of the discussion stops being about the subject matter and starts being about one of you, it's no longer fair or productive. That's my cue to say, "I have reached a point where I can no longer be nice. I'm too [angry/hurt/ready to throttle you] to continue, so I need to table this and come back to finish the discussion in [20 minutes/an hour/when hell freezes over]."

It really doesn't matter whether the other person wants to keep going, if one of you has realized that the fight is getting dirty, you owe it to yourself to back away. (Of course, if we were any good at this naturally, we might not be divorcing. I see and concede the irony.) The key is to keep your promise to return to the table after the timeout in order to make progress.

That bears repeating: *you must return, as promised, to the table.* It's amazing how a cool-off period can clarify your position on who "deserves" the stepladder or how critical it is to win every point because the OP CHEATED ON YOU AND OWES YOU EVERYTHING, THE LYING SCUM.

You both know why you're divorcing and that you're probably not changing your minds, so all that came before is largely irrelevant; what matters is how well you are learning to manage conflict and how you're teaching your children to handle conflict in difficult circumstances.

While you may try to shield them from nastiness under normal circumstances, it's very hard to be so disciplined when it's during a divorce and you *know* you are in the right. Trust me, both of you think that the OP is wrong. In fact, the conviction that the OP is wrong may sometimes be the only thing on which you can reach agreement. How's that for a brainteaser? You're never going to win an argument with mutually exclusive goals and convictions.

Again, you don't always get what's fair; you get what you can agree to, hopefully without fighting dirty. I don't care how much pride you have to swallow; I care that you are being a good role model.

If you're not convinced yet, wait and see how thoroughly it undermines your own ability to broker arguments between your children if the grownups can't do any better.

20

Keep It Off Facebook!

Anything you say can (and probably will) be used against you in a court of law.

Facebook, email, texts, and recorded voice mails are loaded material. Once they are out, you cannot take them back. If you don't want any of it used against you, don't publish it!

It's also rude and bad etiquette to disrespect an ex-partner on social media. You will regret it, either when you cool down or when you face up to it in a legal skirmish.

Plus? It can be part of the discovery process! As Richard Adams warns in "Facebook a top cause of relationship trouble, say US lawyers" (http://bit.ly/gvJLtj):[4]

> Even though the rate of divorce in the US has remained largely stable in recent years, American divorce lawyers and academics [are] picking out Facebook as a leading cause of relationship trouble, with American lawyers now demanding to see their clients' Facebook pages as a matter of course before the start of proceedings.
>
> "...One spouse connects online with someone they knew from school. The person is emotionally available and they start communicating through Facebook," said Dr. Steven Kimmons, a clinical psychologist and marriage counselor at Loyola University Medical Centre near Chicago... A 2010 survey by the American Academy of Matrimonial Lawyers (AAML) found that four out of five lawyers reported an increasing

4. www.guardian.co.uk/technology/2011/mar/08/facebook-us-divorces

number of divorce cases citing evidence derived from social networking sites in the past five years, with Facebook being the market leader…

Photographs harvested from social networking sites… are a particularly rich source of damning evidence, according to divorce lawyers.

Both my husband and I have blocked his OP from our Facebook profiles and adjusted our privacy settings. We haven't done the same for my OP because we are all friends. We are kind to one another online, share funny stories, and are "friends" with each other's parents. You have to be absolutely sure you can stay on the high road or lock down all your privacy settings. I am SO not kidding.

It gets scarier. Get a load of this article by Leanne Italie from MSNBC: "Facebook is divorce lawyers' new best friend."[5] WHAT? Argh!

Forgot to de-friend your wife on Facebook while posting vacation shots of your mistress?

Her divorce lawyer will be thrilled.

Oversharing on social networks has led to an overabundance of evidence in divorce cases. The American Academy of Matrimonial Lawyers says 81 percent of its members have used or faced evidence plucked from Facebook, MySpace, Twitter and other social networking sites, including YouTube and LinkedIn, over the last five years…

- Husband goes on Match.com and declares his single, childless status while seeking primary custody of said nonexistent children.
- Husband denies anger management issues but posts on Facebook in his "write something about yourself" section: "If you have the balls to get in my face, I'll kick your ass into submission."
- Father seeks custody of the kids, claiming (among other things) that his ex-wife never attends the events of their young ones. Subpoenaed evidence from the gaming site World of Warcraft tracks her there with her boyfriend at the precise time she was supposed to be out with the children. Mom loves Facebook's Farmville, too, at all the wrong times.
- Mom denies in court that she smokes marijuana but posts partying, pot-smoking photos of herself on Facebook.

"… You're finding information that you just never get in the normal discovery process—ever," Leslie Matthews said. "People are just blabbing things all over Facebook. People don't yet quite connect what they're saying in their divorce cases is completely different from what they're saying on Facebook. It doesn't even occur to them that they'd be found out…"

If you aren't scared straight by now, you aren't paying close enough attention.

---

5. http://nbcnews.to/NrLQ20
   www.msnbc.msn.com/id/37986320/ns/technology_and_science-tech_and_gadge
   ts/t/facebook-divorce-lawyers-new-best-friend/#.T_iTvXDzf9Qx

21 You Will Make Frenemies

Take everything under advisement and then act from your head and your heart. Others will want to relive their experience through you.

Here's one of the trickiest parts to struggling through a divorce: deciding whom to trust.

You are suddenly down to half your parenting team, right when you have to make some pretty scary and important decisions. Family and friends will rush in to offer opinions for every decision you need to make, coming down ever so slightly (or with a thud) on either your side or the OP's. You hope you have your share of supporters. Maybe you will and maybe you won't.

Friends and family have great capacity to cross over into frenemy territory. I like Urban Dictionary's definitions of frenemy:[6]

- An enemy disguised as a friend.
- The type of "friend" whose words or actions bring you down... they're good people that you can count on to bring you down again sometime in the near future...Straighten 'em out or leave them.
- Someone who is both friend and enemy, a relationship that is both mutually beneficial and dependent while being competitive, fraught with risk and mistrust.
- Someone who you pretend to like but really, you both know you hate each other.
- A "friend"... who cares only about themselves...One might stay in a "frenemy" situation because they are fearful of this person. Also known as a toxic friendship.
- A person with whom you may have a lot of fun and/or a lot in common, who also has a vile and random dark side... you will

6. http://urbandictionary.com/define.php?term=frenemy

probably become their frenemy as well—because you won't be able to keep from talking behind their back... It is recommended for your own safety/sanity that you limit yourself to one frenemy at any given time in your life.

You need to be able to finger frenemies.

Some folks don't even know they are the frenemy. They think they are helping because they believe they know best. They try to gain the confidence of all parties. Everyone likes to be on the inside, and it's tempting to imagine oneself the confidant of *both* sides. A frenemy may think she knows both sides and play you against one another. Or, he may think he knows what's best, and steer you both toward his own personal goal, while he persists in thinking it's the mutual goal. Or, worse, she may unconsciously be rectifying some of her own mistakes by influencing your process. Confide if you must, but be very careful what information gets out there that could hurt you or your family, or, worse, be used against you by the OP. Don't break Rule 5 by revealing too much of your story.

A more insidious form of frenemy is someone who has been a part of your life for some time (oh, say, your best friend) and moves in to console your OP.

True story (and this underscores the futility of hiding information): A divorcing parent had difficulty getting the OP to produce bank and credit card statements even though it was a routine part of the disclosure process. Months went by with repeated requests costing a fortune in attorney's fees. In the end, the OP couldn't avoid disclosure, and so a confession came with it. It turns out that a credit card had been used to fly that "best friend" out for a tryst. It *had* to be confessed, because that friend's name was *right there on the statement*. It goes to show that in the Information Age, every bit of data can work for or against you.

Get Therapy from a Therapist, Not Your Attorney—It's Cheaper

In court, it's not what is right or fair, it's what you can prove.

A lawyer is not a therapist, and a courtroom is not a group session. You will never get emotional satisfaction from a court proceeding. You will get a ruling. It's not what's fair; it's what you can prove. Keep your detachment about who and what your lawyer really is. If you hope to get any sort of closure in court, you could be sorely disappointed.

The court will decide based upon what can be proven, but what you can do is find other ways to have that cathartic release. Confide in a friend. Find online support groups. Indulge in primal scream therapy. Make angry iTunes playlists. (In the appendices, see "Divorce Playlists" and "Online Divorce Support Communities" for some great recommendations.)

Or, try my favorite: learn from other's well-intentioned mistakes. I find it fascinating to read about the stupid, stupid things people do and say and tell themselves to justify horrific behavior during and after a divorce. I mean, look at the OP. There was a time when you couldn't live without the OP. You just HAD to have him. And now you're wondering, what was wrong with me? How in the name of little green apples can this person to whom I pledged my troth be capable of such behavior? Where was my judgment? Why didn't anybody stop me? WHAT IS GOING ON?

You're growing up, that's what's going on. Recognizing and owning up to mistakes and misconceptions and our own parts in the disintegration of the marriage are vital to our *making things better from now on*. That's what we're shooting for, am I right? We can't change the past, but let's shape the future. In order to do that, you have to be open to new perspectives, and be willing to absorb the learning that others have glossed over. There is nothing so dangerous as magical thinking, except for maybe willful ignorance. I think they may be opposite sides of the same coin; whatever. It's a bad penny! Don't pick it up!

I have heard about nightmare divorces where thousands of dollars were spent arguing over a $10 cutting board. Again, I think this goes back to fighting fair. And, of course, being a bit rational.

Going through your lawyer isn't always rational. As they say, when all you have is a hammer, everything starts to look like a nail. Complain to a lawyer, and he will want to take legal action. Diane Holcombe, RN and Life and Wellness Coach (Supporting You Through Transitions at http://www.clarifyyou.com), has this to say:

> A lawyer will say, "Call me—call me about anything," while they are blindsiding you with charges and at the same [adding] fire to the flame. If you say, "I'm upset because OP didn't bring the kids home on time again," the attorney will say, "That's inexcusable, we will hold OP in contempt! You have an agreement, OP can't do that, we will stop him, OP will have to answer for that, OP will have to pay the fees because OP will be in contempt," etc., etc., etc. Five thousand dollars in, you find out that judges don't really like to hold anyone in contempt these days… [all the while] you're just trying to have some lines drawn so your children come home when they are supposed to.

> I cannot stress enough that you need to attempt mediation before lawyers. Lawyers will only take your money and increase the hostility.

Work it out with a smart therapist. Your lawyer will be happy to listen to you go on and on for $350 an hour, but, again, that's more to his or her benefit, not to yours.

Part IV
Getting Down to Business—the Process

You are only going to get one first chance to settle the major financial and administrative aspects of your divorce. You can mutually agree to a change after the fact, of course, but I really, really, really suggest you get to acceptable NOW. Also? Your children are watching and learning how to behave in a crisis: with integrity or deceit; grace or malice. Choose wisely and use your powers for good.

- Rule 23: Get Familiar with Your Own Psychological State
- Rule 24: Disclose the Real Financial Picture and Agree on What to Preserve
- Rule 25: Be It Ever So Fleeting, There Is No Thing Like Court-Ordered Support
- Rule 26: Empathy Is the Most Important Tool In Your Co-Parenting Toolkit
- Rule 27: Set Up a Predictable Routine and Agree on How to Change It
- Rule 28: Choose a Scheduling Tool That You Can Both Understand and Use
- Rule 29: Use Child Support for the Children
- Rule 30: Help Your Kids Develop a Process for Transferring between Houses

Every reunion with one parent is also a separation with the other; each "hello" is also a "goodbye."
—Jocelyn Block, MA. and Melinda Smith, MA.

23 Get Familiar with Your Own Psychological State

Self-actualization is NOT for when you're down in the trenches.

You are in crisis mode. Some days it will feel overwhelming, and others you may be able to compartmentalize enough to take a deep breath. There are so many balls in the air—psychological, practical, and emotional, never mind financial—that it helps to break things down into terms you can understand and use to help others grasp how you feel and how they can (or can't) help.

I was a child of divorce, and I hated it. I hated that my dad lived two states away and that we only saw him on alternate holidays and for several weeks during the summer. I hated not having memories of my parents together. I loved them both so much, how could they not like each other? It felt like a trick question. Looking back, I see that they were doing what they had to do to survive. They had to take it one step at a time, beginning with basic safety and progressing to a point where everyone could start to heal and finally accept and embrace the changes. There was a progressive hierarchy of needs.

There is a psychological construct that has guided me through life that breaks down these needs into understandable, distinct segments. It's something I'd like you to give some serious thought to and keep on a permanent shelf in your brain. This construct is called Maslow's Hierarchy of Needs (http://bit.ly/iWlvvW).[7]

---

7. en.wikipedia.org/wiki/Maslow's_hierarchy_of_needs

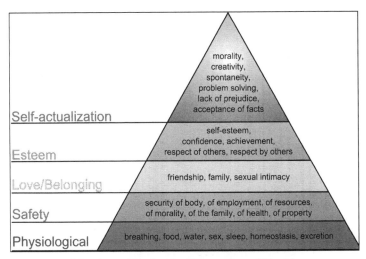

Abraham Maslow's Hierarchy of Needs

Here's a crash course in Abraham Maslow's Hierarchy of Needs:

This hierarchy is most often displayed as a pyramid. The lowest levels of the pyramid are made up of the most basic needs, while the more complex needs are located at the top of the pyramid. Needs at the bottom of the pyramid are basic physical require-ments including the need for food, water, sleep, and warmth. Once these lower-level needs have been met, people can move on to the next level of needs, which are for safety and security.

As people progress up the pyramid, needs become increasingly psychological and social. Soon, the need for love, friendship, and intimacy become important. Further up the pyramid, the need for personal esteem and feelings of accomplishment take priority... Maslow emphasized the importance of self-actualization, which is a process of growing and developing as a person in order to achieve individual potential.

Self-actualization is NOT for when you're down in the trenches. People will try to help "uplift" you, but right now you're in the shit and you just need to survive. Cover the basics in that lowest level. Then think about the next level. You may not see the top of that pyramid for a while, and that's OK. It's not a luxury you can afford until you are finished with the process (which could be never) or are independently wealthy (again, possibly never, in the case of divorce).

You may feel like you're spending an inordinate amount of time in the lower levels of Maslow's Triangle. I've lived in that basement-level apartment myself for longer stretches than I'd like to admit. I call it "Re-decorating Maslow's Basement." Put up some drapes, throw down a rug, paint the walls, do some fucking thing, because we're going to be here a while. Might as well make it homey.

24

Disclose the Real Financial Picture and Agree on What to Preserve

You will feel like an asshole if you eventually have to admit to your kids that you pissed away the college funds in a bitter court battle.

Assets are incredibly important. You need to protect them! The more you spend on lawyers, retail therapy, and revenge splurging, the less you will have for what really matters.

Maintain discipline—in fact, put more discipline in place than ever before—because you will need the money in ways you cannot possibly imagine right now. Suck it up. Sit down together to take inventory and list everything: cash, 401Ks, IRAs, stocks and options, the car(s), net equity in your home, cash value of insurance policies, and *anything* else of value. Concentrate only on tangible assets. No need right now to argue the relative value of that antique sideboard or Fido. That's for property division time.

Once you have an idea of the net assets, you can start to discuss what you'd like to see left standing once the dust settles. Want the kids to go to college? Agree not to touch anything you've set aside for that purpose.

Want to be able to retire or at least have a cushion for the future that will support you if social security fails? Don't cash in and spend your retirement accounts if you are under 59 ½! The institutions will withhold taxes at your current tax rate, plus a 10 percent penalty.

Want to be able to buy groceries, medicine, gas, and school clothes? Don't rack up the credit card debt—it will only worsen your individual credit rating. Yes, you will now have to qualify for loans, housing, etc. on your own, a certainty that will make it harder to get back on your feet when the dust settles.

Want to keep in the good graces of your legal team? Follow advice. If you have legal bills you can't pay after all is over, you can be sued by your lawyer for nonpayment of fees. Your lawyer may fight like a lion for you right up until the settlement, but after that, it's his or her own interests that need protecting. Never stiff your lawyer: you may end up back in court, because things often happen *about* divorce *after* the divorce. Bringing a new legal representative up to speed will cost much, much more than if you are able to pull your original team off the bench.

You may have to work harder now to keep yourself and your family afloat. The OP has to work harder too because you've got two households to maintain. Moreover, the children need to feel safe in both places, which means providing equal comfort in each household to the greatest extent possible.

I know this sounds dismal, and it is. There is no way to come through a divorce financially intact. No matter how much either of you earns or has stashed away, you will never again have the benefit of shared expenses.

I'll tell you this for free: anything you do to shortchange the other household will just make you look like a jerk. Maybe not today, maybe not this year, but it will when the kids are old enough to understand why you aren't married anymore. And, then, if there aren't any funds to educate the children, you will feel like an asshole if you have to admit that you pissed away their college funds in a bitter court battle. Think of all the money that could still be there, with compound interest. Was it really worth bankrupting the marital assets?

25

Be It Ever So Fleeting, There Is No Thing Like Court-Ordered Support

There's nothing like support. Sometimes, it's literally nothing.

Child support is a bizarre little animal, designed to protect each party in a divorce. In case you skipped the page where I say I'm not a doctor, lawyer, psychiatrist, pharmacist, or judge: seek legal counsel if you have questions about support.

There's nothing like support. Sometimes, it's literally nothing. The norm, at least in California where I divorced, is for support to last about half the length of the marriage. That is a SWAG*, people, don't hold me to it.

Oddly, as I was typing "SWAG," my cell rang. It was a manager with whom I'd worked twenty-two years ago. He divorced with dignity and grace, and his kids were all over eighteen years old and on their own. That means he's done paying child support, right? His OP had not planned for that eventuality. He told me, "She was an idiot not to have known that child support would end the day the last child came of age, but I didn't want her to be homeless, so I paid her, in cash, for about another year and a half."

He's a Prince Reliable, helping her out for the good of the family. The OP is, after all, still the mother or father of your children. But the responsibility spectrum is broad. Some bankrupt the OP in court, use the children as pawns in negotiations, exaggerate needs to get the upper hand in a settlement, or tell children things they should never hear to garner loyalty or build distrust in the OP. I know the people in these stories but would not identify them for all the gold in Mike Tyson's teeth:

Sophisticated Wild Ass Guess.

- A stay-at-home dad pressed kidnapping charges while the OP had the kids for visitation.
- A couple couldn't agree on a child's name. The boy is Tom in one house and Harry in the other.
- A mother exaggerated her children's special needs to justify never returning to the workforce.
- A man left his executive position for a minimum-wage job so he wouldn't have to pay support. He now lives with (or rather, off) his girlfriend.
- A wife agreed to move the family 2,000 miles for her husband's new job, then announced that she was staying behind with the children and her high school boyfriend with whom she'd reconnected on Facebook. Oh, and she was having his baby.
- A man took his wife away for one last night of romance a few weeks before their second child was born. He wined and dined her and made love to her. The next day he told her that he was moving in with his secretary and that he only wanted shared custody of the first child.

Others agree to pay support and at some point don't. Legitimate reasons may arise for not being able to honor a support agreement. In those cases, hightail it to court and file for cessation, establishing a basis for resumption once circumstances normalize. If you don't, you will continue to owe every month! Without a precise support agreement on record, you are screwed.

Here's the sorry secret: support accrues with interest and cannot be discharged except by mutual agreement. Not even bankruptcy can erase a support obligation. The smart ones do not play games with the law. Others will be sued, have their wages garnisheed, or be jailed for nonpayment. It's bad all around for everyone. A parent depending on support is suddenly left without that income. A parent may lose his or her job, but the children may lose food and shelter. If you sue the OP, you are suing your children. Both parents incur legal fees that take food out of their kids' mouths and higher education off the table.

This isn't about the parents; it's about the children. Be Prince Reliable or Princess Dependable. Your children are taking mental notes.

26 Empathy Is the Most Important Tool in Your Co-Parenting Toolkit

Even when you and the OP agree on how things should work, it's easy to get tangled in the details.

Establishing and taming routines will either be the easiest portion or the hardest part of your divorce. There seems to be no middle ground on this; it's binary. In my experience—and I have spent so much time thinking about this it's hair-tearingly ridiculous—there are two types of people when it comes to custody schedules:

1. A person comfortable with routine and with a great capacity for empathy; and

2. A person who will constantly change times, places, and dates without always clearly communicating those changes.

I could be wrong, but I believe the difference between those two types boils down to the capacity for empathy. You could argue with me that it's consideration, personality type, or any other aspect of a person's psyche, but I will maintain that it is the individual's capacity for empathy.

Em·pa·thy noun   /'em-pə-thē/◄)

the action of understanding, being aware of, being sensitive to, and vicariously experiencing the feelings, thoughts, and experience of another of either the past or present without having the feelings, thoughts, and experience fully communicated in an objectively explicit manner; also: the capacity for empathy.[8]

---

8. http://www.merriam-webster.com/medical/empathy

In a nutshell, people in that second category may have a marked lack of regret and shame, or at least be unable to acknowledge those feelings.

(Pardon my detour into definitions. Before I really got a handle on what made people in that second category tick, I was having an endless dialogue in my head, wondering how someone could THINK of operating that way. Don't they SEE what it does to others? WHAT IN HELL makes them think this is in any way productive? But I digress. Deeeep breath.)

Even when you and the OP agree on how things should work, it's easy to get tangled in the details: the daily execution, changes to schedules, dropping off and picking up the children, and communicating changes to the agreement. It can keep you in a state of constant catch-up and discombobulation. Or maybe that's just me, but I don't think so.

So, you start by getting help from a mediator (if that's the route you take, please, please, let it be that route) that specializes in custody and related scheduling issues. If you are able to agree on a co-parenting plan, you will walk out of that office with a document known as some variation of a "Child Custody and Visitation Stipulation" that is contained in your "Divorce Memorandum of Understanding."

Rule 27 will help you actually go about constructing and implementing your co-parenting plan. One last caveat: do not, under any circumstances, agree to "wing it." Not even as a gesture of trust and good will. The documents and the law are there to protect everyone involved, and serve as THE word on what is decreed. If there is any disagreement in the future about custody schedules or financial support, you've got to be able to refer back to a document you BOTH signed. You can change your co-parenting plan or support agreement at any time with mutual consent at a very low cost—maybe an hour of a paralegal's time plus filing fee. (Again I'm not a lawyer; please consult for your area.) There is no good reason to make side deals (except for one-offs or ad hoc favors), especially if the deal is called off by one of you and the agreement is not mutual. Your side deal will mean nothing if it's not part of the official record.

In real estate, it's location, location, location. In divorce, it's paper trail, paper trail, paper trail.

27 Set Up a Predictable Routine and Agree on How to Change It

A schedule is a tool, not a weapon.

Here's a paradigm shift for you: the romantic relationship that was meant to last forever has just become an evergreen business partnership. It doesn't hurt to treat it like one; it's certainly as important and needs to be taken seriously.

When you create your custody and visitation agreement, make sure you cover the following areas:

- Primary residence and percentage of custody.
- The weekly schedule for each child and how it dovetails with the custody schedule.
- Holidays, birthdays, summer vacations, and coverage of personal vacation time.
- Protocol and timing for dropping off and picking up the children: who does the driving and where is the transfer location (i.e., custodial parent drops off at the OP's home vs. meeting half way between houses).
- Activities, who pays for them, and who is responsible for transportation.
- Information exchange, e.g., copies of homework and accolades, notices about parent teacher conferences, permission slips, etc. (You may be able to get the school to send announcements to both homes, or better yet, have both parents' email addresses included in announcements/blasts.) I myself sometimes resort to photocopying things I discover at the OP's house, but not in a criminal fashion. Besides, no jury would convict me.

- Procedure for how all major decisions regarding the children are made, such as authorization of non-emergency medical treatment, child counseling, religious decisions, education, and school choices.
- How extra expenses will be split for sports, tutoring, medical deductibles, and other expenses, as well as sitter expenses for when one of you is in school or at work.
- Process for resolving conflicts should any arise.

You and the OP need to agree how to handle each of these scenarios. I can't even pretend to have covered all the variations, as it can be mind-boggling once your children are in school and have activities. Fortunately, these details can be worked out with the mediator, who has probably seen it all and will have helpful suggestions. Remember, a schedule is a tool, not a weapon. Hammering out an agreement in front of a third party and getting it all in writing will help ensure compliance.

Those are the logistics. You'll also need to set ground rules for parent behavior, to wit:

- Non-Disparagement: no disparaging remarks or comments made in front of the children about your ex-spouse or any significant other person in their lives.
- Right of First Refusal to Provide Care, that is, if you have another obligation during your time with the children, you give the OP say forty-eight hours (if possible) to take the children during this period instead of getting a sitter. If the OP does not want to or cannot take the children, it is the custodial parent's full responsibility to get care for the children during this period.
- Modifications to this Agreement, i.e., how to change the document and how to process disagreements prior to resorting to going to court for relief.

If you've already had experience with this, you may be laughing at me right now. I should talk. Our custody schedule is clear, but the execution sometimes flops like a dying marlin.

Bottom line: the better the two of you get at sharing responsibility for these activities, the less stress you will have and the less stress the children will be under in an already difficult situation. They didn't ask for two houses, two schedules, and two sets of house rules, and they didn't ask to split their time with the two most important people in their lives. It is your job to put aside your personal feelings and find a workable agreement and to make that agreement work for everyone involved.

28 Choose a Scheduling Tool That You Can Both Understand and Use

Usability = the skill level of each party + the willingness of each party to use those skills.

A schedule is useless unless all parties agree to, are aware of, and follow it. There is a list of some great scheduling and management tools in the appendices; go check them out after you've absorbed Rules 26 and 27. Co-parenting from separate domiciles adds a level of communication that is qualitatively different from communicating while living in the same house. Communicating across domiciles is more formal; however, it feels less controlled and more like a business partnership to manage the information flow about constantly changing schedules involving dentists, doctors, sports, work, play, and school.

So! You have a parenting plan and you think you are all set. Not even close. All of those items in that parenting plan need to be communicated and confirmed so that both parents know who, what, when, where, and why. You will have legal issues, money issues, and issues you can't begin to guess at now. At times, the last thing you want to do is communicate with this person, even for the kids. Get over it.

There are many options, but both of you have to agree to use the tool. There is a whole industry dedicated to this process, and your court/judge could even mandate a tool/process if communication is a significant problem. No parenting plan is complete unless it includes HOW communication will take place and with what tool. Sometimes getting the OP to use the tool is the hardest part, so try to get that into the parenting plan.

My personal favorite is a tool called OurFamilyWizard.com. It is not free but allows for excellent tracking of dates, daily routines, medical information, journals, expense logs (to track expenses to be paid by the OP or shared), message boards, etc. Other tools, such as Google Calendar or Cozi.com, also work but function only as a calendar and do not store additional items. Email provides a trail, and spreadsheets are easy to use but don't store the information in one place, and you are forever trying to make sure the OP agrees, receives the information, or updates the details.

My husband keeps a master Google Calendar for his kids, displays it next to his business calendar, and stores all emails and finance/expenses in a folder for 'proof' verification. I would shoot myself in the head if I had to do all that. I finally convinced him to use OurFamilyWizard.com. It would save the family time and keep important documents from both parents about the kids in one location. It seems like my poor husband is forever verifying and being proactive while his OP communicates when the mood strikes.

Amazingly, sometimes the OP has difficulty remembering that this is all about the kids. Having a centralized repository for information on appointments, along with journal information (daily updates on issues or happy moments), allows the kids to enjoy being kids without being dragged into their parents' inefficient, volatile, or hostile handling of administrative tasks.

My partner's OP won't use Google Calendar or any other online calendar, so they are left with email, text messages, and brief words being exchanged when the children are dropped off. One thing that did work for a while was a notebook that was always kept in the kids' backpacks. Now those notebooks are gone, but occasional notes are still used.

In short, the right tool will let you know exactly what, when, where, who, and why. It will leave a paper trail. It lets you know what's happening when you are not with the kids, and it will make them feel more secure knowing they don't have to be in the crossfire of verbal communication over calendar items when being dropped off.

Usability = the skill level of each party + the willingness of each party to use those skills. For some examples of excellent co-parenting calendars and tools, see the appendix: "Family Scheduling Tools."

29 Use Child Support for the Children

Child support is for a child's living expenses and health insurance. I am so not kidding; I will hunt you down and shame you into accepting this if I have to.

There is so much to be said on this subject that I can only cover a few things and then refer you to resources in the appendices. Therefore, please imagine me standing in front of you in the kitchen, waving a glass of wine, and pounding my fist on the counter while saying the following: **child support is for a child's living expenses and health insurance. I am so not kidding; I will hunt you down and shame you into accepting this if I have to.**

Here are some brainteasers:

- A parent pays support to the OP, who then purchases clothing or gifts for the children. The OP insists that these expenses should be split. No, one might say, the first parent has already paid 100 percent of said expenses. "Splitting" would mean the parent pays *150 percent* of those expenses. Don't ask for what you already have.
- A parent pays support to the OP that totals roughly double what the rent and utilities cost, yet the OP is always broke. What is the OP spending the child support on, if not on the children?
- A parent supports his children and the OP, who does not work. The OP adopts new, expensive hobbies and is always dressed in expensive clothes and shoes. The children, however, often don't have clothes or shoes that fit or basic school supplies. Legally, the paying parent has NO SAY OR CONTROL over how child support is spent. Legally, nothing can or should be done. Morally, it is wrong, wrong, wrong.

I try not to judge, but these things make me very, very judgy. It's about the kids, people, not you! Revenge spending or selfish indulgence is not good for the kids.

Heh, about two dozen people are immediately going to think I am talking about them. I'm not talking about you!! I am piecing together separate, anonymous examples to give flavor to the points I'm making. That doesn't mean I'm exaggerating. I'm not kidding when I say I've seen things that make me want to claw my eyes out.

So!

From here on out, I'll stick to technical issues. Again, please get proper legal advice; I am not qualified to give it. I am merely working with what I consider to be reliable sources and my own (and anonymous contributors') first-hand experiences.

The following excerpts are direct from the *State of CA Child Support Handbook*:

What is Child Support?

Both parents have the legal duty to provide financial support for their child. Child support is money paid by both parents to meet their child's living and medical expenses.

...Child support is for ordinary living expenses. It does not pay childcare, medical bills not paid by insurance, travel costs of visitation, or special education needs.

Things that can happen if you do not pay voluntary child support as ordered, according to the *Handbook*:

- Your credit rating can be affected.
- If you declare bankruptcy, it does not mean you do not still owe child support. Such a filing CANNOT discharge child support.
- You may be denied a passport until you are completely current with payments.
- A lien may be filed against your real property, if any.
- Your driver's license may be suspended.
- The Franchise Tax Board, if alerted by Child Support Services, can TAKE FUNDS from bank accounts, rental incomes, royalties, dividends, and commissions, and can intercept tax refunds to pay past due child support.

Also, if you win the lottery or file for unemployment, benefits can be taken to pay both current and past due support. Many parents have collected past due support from the OP's unemployment checks. This is one rare, good thing about the economic bust—attached unemployment benefits have paid out lots of past due support dollars.

In short: take it seriously and follow the law!

30

Help Your Kids Develop a Process for Transferring between Houses

When I'm dead and gone, my headstone will read, "She went back for one too many forgotten items."

I liked this article on DivorceMagazine.com by Isolina Ricci, Ph. D. because it got to the heart of the child's experience of moving between households and how our reactions to their adjustment can help or hinder the process.

> [A] common grumble of parents when children return from being with their OP is that some item —a favorite toy or a jacket—has been left behind. The first, knee-jerk reaction becomes: the OP or the child has been inconsiderate, thoughtless, or deliberately provoking. Actually, this forgetfulness probably stems from the child's need to stake a claim to some territory to create a sense of belonging in his or her newer home...

> Some personal things belong in each home and stay there... The sense of "my own things, here" matters. So does a trust that their things will remain protected in their absence.[9]

Ohhhh, the forgotten item. When I'm dead and gone, my headstone will read, "She went back for one too many forgotten items."

Create individual survival kits that go with the kids wherever they go. It can be their backpack; it can be an additional bag. That kit goes wherever the kid goes.

For instance, my kids know when it's time to go to dad's, it means they need to:

---

9. http://bit.ly/wdk72h
   www.divorcemag.com/articles/Children_and_Divorce/
   momdadhouse.html

- Repack all papers, textbooks, and supplies necessary to do schoolwork in class and homework at home;
- Gather all video games, etc., PLUS all chargers. Also? Ear buds. Buy extras.
- Pack lovies, blankets, books, favorite jackets, favorite jammies, etc.
- Take OUT any items that "live" at one house and should not be transferred to the other house. For us, this means Nerf guns do not come to our house and iPods do not go to the other house.
- Cell phone and charger.

About that cell phone: if your children are old enough, consider giving them each a cell phone. It can be a cheap, dial-only phone with your number(s) pre-programmed in it. This is controversial, I know, but I think divorce changes the rules a bit. I need to know that I can reach my children, and they need to know that they can reach me, without having to go through the OP. You may not think this could be a problem, but really, how would you know? By definition, you're not hearing about it. Personal cell phones also come in handy when the kids are at a friend's house, a practice, or school and need to be picked up if the OP can't be reached.

My favorite part of having an all-cell-phone family is that I can track the whereabouts of each child online (or at least their phones). Your phone carrier may offer a "Family Map" GPS tracking service. As an example, iPhones have a feature called Find My iPhone that will pinpoint the location of the phone and let you send an alert sound and message to that phone. If it is lost or stolen, you can remotely lock the phone, or even wipe it clean to prevent access to personal data.

Consider keeping a notebook that lives in the child's backpack in which parents write down how the time went, what they did, any issues, news, or discipline issues (see my stance on that in Rule 13). This is a way for parents to NOT HAVE TO TALK during a transfer if civil communication is an issue. My partner and his OP kept notebooks for about a year, until everyone was comfortable with the routine and communication improved to the point where it wasn't necessary.

If there are medications, there should be a medicine bag that is always personally handed to the OP. The child should not suffer lack of necessary medications because a parent forgot them, and this is the one item parents should return for if forgotten, no matter what, without complaint.

Part V
Regaining and Preserving Sanity (and Being a Good Parent to Boot)

This section deals with what you may need most at this time, but are least likely to pursue. You may not feel like taking care of yourself, you may feel that the anger and resentment will never let you rest, and you may seek comfort by—well, let's just say that there are a few things that won't promote your sense of well-being.

- Rule 31: Make Taking Care of Yourself a Priority
- Rule 32: Take Your Temperature on Resentment Early and Often
- Rule 33: Do Not Sleep with the OP

I feel angry but not homicidal; this may be un-looked-for progress.
—Suzanne Finnamore, *Split: A Memoir of Divorce*

31 Make Taking Care of Yourself a Priority

Just the effort will make you feel like someone cares, even if it's only you who cares.

I am not very good at this rule, and I'm betting you aren't either. Get with it. You're working your way to being single, so any spousal support system you might have had is going away.

What will take its place? People around you will want to help, but they can't know what's best for you in all circumstances. Sometimes you need to cry. Have ice cream. Watch old movies. Fall in love with a snugly blanket when you need to cocoon, which will happen suddenly and at odd hours. No one else will be able to give you exactly what you need, when you need it.

You need to find your own ways to make yourself a priority. Maybe taking yoga classes would help (I never did this myself, against all evidence supporting its efficacy in soothing body and mind—I'm stubborn that way). Or maybe finding a hobby, or going to the movies alone would help. I could go on, but there are other books with better advice on prioritizing yourself. I haven't quite got there yet myself.

The rule is that you take care of you, to be able to take care of your children, on top of everything else that comes with running a household all by yourself. You need to get out of your head, however you can.

I got an earful to this effect from a friend who was a wonderful sounding board for me through my divorce. He wasn't close enough to be able to slap me out of it, so he sent a note. (Thank you, by the way.)

Listen very carefully, Mindy: You have had several major life changes in the last few months. If you don't let yourself get over these without beating yourself up, you will do yourself irreparable harm. You have:

- Divorced;
- Left your job;
- Been parted from your work friends;
- Started a new relationship;
- Discovered a lump in your breast;
- Lost several friends; Etc., etc., etc.

Give yourself a break, woman. You are in no state to be making major decisions, certainly not ones that will affect your life or the lives of your kids. Please let your friends help you. Please, please listen to advice and take your time weighing it before making a decision. Accept that there are people who love you dearly and are willing to do anything they can to help you even if the advice isn't what you want to hear. And please ease the fuck off on yourself. You can't do everything all at once, Mindy. You need to learn this new role bit by bit. The first, the FIRST thing you need to do is focus on your kids and make this new dynamic work for all of you. The kids are just learning how to deal with all the changes, so they are acting out. It will take all of your time. You are their life, so you protect yourself and cocoon your family in love and warmth. THAT is your priority, baby, always.

I now make it a point to get out of my head when I start spinning up. I read a book, watch a movie, listen to music, take a drive, or treat myself to a bubble bath with a glass of wine. It doesn't always work, but it works better than doing nothing. Just the effort will make you feel like someone cares, even if it's only you who cares.

32 Take Your Temperature on Resentment Early and Often

If I could sell the feeling of relief when one lets go of resentment, I could buy and sell Bill Gates twice a week just for giggles.

We're going to concentrate on definitions here because they are crafted by people smarter than I am. I just taught you a trick there: It's often best to quote others when dealing with the OP. Experts know what they're talking about; you make gnat-like buzzing sounds.

Resentment and denial are BFFs. One denies resentment, then resents implications of denial, and then—you get the picture.

> Resentment (also called ranklement or bitterness) is the experience of a negative emotion (anger or hatred, for instance) felt as a result of a real or imagined wrong done. Etymologically, the word originates from French *"ressentir"*, re-, intensive prefix, and *sentir* "to feel"; from the Latin *"sentire"*. The English word has become synonymous with anger, spite, and bitterness.[10]

I particularly like what Wikipedia goes on to say about Alcoholics Anonymous' philosophy around dealing with resentment (http://en.wikipedia.org/wiki/Resentment):

> The Alcoholics Anonymous organization cites resentment as the number one offender, and one of the greatest threats to an alcoholic. **Several of the Twelve Steps of AA involve identifying and dealing with resentment as part of the path toward recovery, including acknowledging one's**

10. http://en.wikipedia.org/wiki/Resentment

own role in resentment and praying for the resentment to be taken away. [Emphasis mine.]

Isn't that awesome? There are only twelve steps, and *several* talk about resentment. Whether or not you agree with AA's methods, they have been working for millions of members for seventy-seven years.[11] I'm not preaching religion; I'm not selling Amway. I'm just sayin'.

Back to Wikipedia (http://en.wikipedia.org/wiki/Resentment)

> Resentment is most powerful when it is felt toward someone whom the individual is close to or intimate with. To have an injury resulting in resentful feelings inflicted by a friend or loved one leaves the individual feeling betrayed as well as resentful, and these feelings can have deep effects.
>
> Resentment is an emotionally debilitating condition that, when unresolved, can have a variety of negative results on the person experiencing it, including touchiness or edginess when thinking of the person resented, denial of anger or hatred against this person, and provocation or anger arousal when this person is recognized positively. It can also have more long-term effects, such as the development of a hostile, cynical, sarcastic attitude that may become a barrier against other healthy relationships, lack of personal and emotional growth, difficulty in self-disclosure, trouble trusting others, loss of self-confidence, and overcompensation.[4] By contrast, resentment does not have any direct negative effects on the person resented, save for the deterioration of the relationship involved.

Got that? Your seething means nothing to the OP. Less than nothing. He or she might even be cheered up at the thought of your shorts in a bunch. People with wedgies make mistakes and are easier to outmaneuver in court. Sorry, I don't have any citations for that, but I bet you a tenth of what my friends have spent on divorce attorney fees that I'm not far off.

I don't have a magic wand. I just want you to be aware of your resentment levels every now and then. I don't remember how long it took me to realize that resentment is a totally one-sided and impotent emotion, but it took quite a while for that to permeate both sides of my brain. I do remember the relief I felt when I realized I just didn't care anymore. I was indifferent.

If I could sell the feeling of relief when one lets go of resentment, I could buy and sell Bill Gates twice a week just for giggles.

---

11. Estimates of A.A. Groups and Members as of January 1, 2012 (http://www.aa.org/en_pdfs/smf-53_en.pdf).

33 Do Not Sleep with the OP

Sex, especially with an ex, is emotionally loaded and fraught with complications and barriers to healing and moving on.

A longtime reader of my blog, The Mommy Blog (themommyblog.com), once wrote to me to say:

> My rules were not something I ever wrote down, but I thought of them on a daily basis to get through the day.
>
> 1. Make life better for my children.
> 2. Be happy and show them life will go on and be ok.
> 3. Try to be amicable with the OP for the sake of the kids.
> 4. Do NOT, for ANY reason, fool around with the OP. *
>
> Towards the last few years of my divorce I was pretty depressed. And, then it got worse as I went through the divorce process. The first three years after the divorce the OP was bitter and made my life difficult on may [sic] occasions. I was overwhelmed so those three rules above were a daily challenge (rule four was never a problem, lol). You're so right when you say things will get worse before they get better. But, it did get better. Much better. And, I think it's important for people who are divorcing to remember that. There is a light at the end of the tunnel.
>
> *My OP tried to play this game with me on many different occasions. One time he actually said, and I kid you not, "How about sending me off with a proper good bye?" I must have shot him quite an evil look because he finally stopped trying.

Wait. WHAT? Fool around with the OP? I don't know about you, but when we decided that divorce was inevitable, that was the end of that. We retreated to our separate corners, and I don't know that either of us could stomach the idea of sleeping together, let alone think it was a good idea. Don't get me wrong, I love the guy, he's a wonderful father; we were just a poor match. He agrees. I asked him.

So I thought about this. I asked a few people what they thought about making this a rule. When even my MOTHER said it needed its own rule because it was so important, I threw up my hands and started researching WHY PEOPLE WOULD DO THIS.

And then, quite a few realizations sank in. One was that some people are able to keep sex and emotion compartmentalized to the extent that they can rationalize it as recreational. I personally believe sex, especially with an ex, is emotionally loaded and fraught with complications and barriers to healing and moving on:

- It delays the inevitable and prevents both you and the OP from moving forward. (Natch.)
- There is almost always a catch, real or implied.
- Aren't you lying to yourself, just a little? Not to mention to the OP?
- Sure the OP's not sleeping around? You may be a little too comfortable with having unprotected sex with the one person with whom you've always been able to do that. Is she still on birth control? Sure he's used protection? Sex with the OP is not worth adding an STD to the already long list of reasons you are no longer together. Also? Not a great start for you when you're finally ready to move on with someone new.
- The Mata Hari Syndrome. Are you being too open with your plans and intentions with regard to the divorce? Are you giving away strategies or ammunition that could be used against you in court? Hmmm?
- Are you doing it to exert power?
- Are you doing it to feel important to the OP? Guess what: you already are important, but in new ways. Don't cloud the terms of your new relationship with mixed motivations.

I could go on and on, but all I really care about is that you seriously consider sleeping with the OP a VERY BAD IDEA. For you, for the OP, and for the children.

Part VI
Moving Forward, Taking Care of and Being True to Yourself and Your Children

This section is sort of a Möbius Strip[12] you will be walking along for as long as you and the OP have joint responsibility for the children. The dissolution of a marriage is not the dissolution of a family. You will have good days and bad days, but your best chance for success lies in periodic internal checkups.

Möbius strip

---

12. A Möbius band (or strip) is an intriguing surface with only one side and one edge. You can make one by joining the two ends of a long strip of paper after giving one end a 180-degree twist.An ant can crawl from any point on such a surface to any other point without ever crossing an edge.

- Rule 34: Let It Go: Develop Emotional Callouses
- Rule 35: Be Inclusive!
- Rule 36: Fight Fair and Keep It Civil
- Rule 37: Remember: Children Sense All, See a Lot, and Hear More Than You May Think
- Rule 38: Make a New Template for Relationships
- Rule 39: Your Life Will Be Better after Divorce, or at Least Acceptably Different
- Rule 40: Take Periodic Inventory on Where You Are in the Grief Process
- Rule 41: Keep Hope Alive for Future (Healthier) Relationships
- Rule 42: These Are My Rules. What Are Yours?

Divorce isn't such a tragedy. A tragedy's staying in an unhappy marriage, teaching your children the wrong things about love. Nobody ever died of divorce.
—Jennifer Weiner, Fly Away Home

34

Let It Go: Develop Emotional Callouses

Emotional calluses enable us to let things go.

Emotional calluses enable us to let things go. For the OP and me, thankfully, not very many new bad things have sprung up to replace the original bad things. And now, in my new life, both my partner and I have developed terrific emotional calluses too.

I'm very lucky in my new love. I got to thinking about all the reasons why this second-for-my-partner, third-for-me marriage might just last:

- With six children between the ages of seven and thirteen, we don't have much time to think. And we are always going to need another body on the cleanup crew.
- After having been married and divorced three times between us, perspectives and priorities have been vigorously reshuffled. Emotional calluses have enabled us to let things go. We are in decline with the hanging-onto-things thing and are having a corresponding upswing in tolerance.
- Suddenly a little flirting isn't so irritating. We're secure in one another and know it's not going to lead to threats to the relationship.
- We never, ever want to have to divvy up possessions again with an ex. We don't give a crap about half the stuff we have, so it's doubly exhausting to have to decide its fate.
- Ditto on divvying up the peripherals: very solid reason to stick together, especially if you are a couple of tech geeks with six kids. Chargers are the new record collection.
- The kids are as likely as not to go on with the arrangement without us. They are happy together. They may be perfectly capable of getting along without us. Don't test them.

- We are fully committed to someday purchasing a complete bedding set like the one in a JW Marriott hotel. Saving up could take years.
- We are close in age (proportionately) to our parents and to each other's parents. We like them. They are fun to be around, without all that awkward and pervasive, newly contentious, parent/offspring behavior. Now they are folks we want to have over for dinner and hang out with.
- There really is no reason to talk to the exes beyond housekeeping tasks. I take care of mine, and he takes care of his. Neither of us bitches about the tedium because we know we have evenly distributed the work.
- It is an added bonus that late night and weekend activities do not provoke resentment in one another. We each have our own three-ring circus to manage.
- Vacations aren't much of an issue. Who can fly eight people anywhere? Who would attempt a road trip? How would it even be managed? Better to stay at home where there is never a dull moment. Thank God for Netflix and a pool.
- We both are insanely happy to see each other at the end of the day. Neither of us has ever closed a bedroom door before, let alone locked it, but as zookeepers and wardens know, it's best to have a lockdown until dawn. Individual petitions from the kids can be heard through the doors and dealt with accordingly.

It is comforting to know that there is just as much reason for the head to stay put as there is for the heart, thanks in part to those emotional calluses. I love my partner to distraction—something I hadn't dared to hope for at this stage in life—but I am also comforted by the permanence that is practically guaranteed because we don't want to sort out the iPod cords.

Bottom line: prepare to be sometimes blind and sometimes deaf. Judgments about the OP or his or her methods are inappropriate unless there is something illegal, immoral, or dangerous going on.

It's easier to retain and prune slowly than it is to cut people off and add them back in.

Holidays can be the pits after a divorce. You may not want to be in the same room together, but your children probably want to be with both of you and everyone else in the extended family. You'll have hard decisions to make about how you spend occasions that only accentuate the painful separateness of families of divorce. If you have only a limited capacity for civility toward one another, lavish it on your children with special occasions together.

Sometimes it's not up to you. The in-laws may decide they don't want you around. I can tell you firsthand that's very painful. We were a family for fifteen years. How could I not care about my nieces and nephews and brothers-in-law and sisters-in-law? I was absolutely sick when I stopped being able to see them. But both sides have to want to be inclusive. When I finally got added back in years later, sort of (at a hugely extended family gathering at my parents' home with exes all around), it was awkward trying to undo the deed.

That is why my parents and I have always made sure that the OP has an open invitation to family gatherings. The kids are deliriously happy to have us both there, and that helps us stifle any remnants of hostility. It is not easy, but it beats the snot out of having to eat humble pie later to ask someone back in after they've been shunned.

If the holidays are about getting the family together and seeing friends and showering the kids with candy and gifts and eating too much pie, then I'd say we did the holidays proud this year. We had Christmas dinner at my mom's with my husband and his parents; the OP and his parents, brother, and sister-in-law; our kids; and some friends. If that's not pulling the factions together and saying "Oh yeah? You think so?" to conventional post-divorce social norms, I don't know what is.

This inclusiveness rule underscores the rule to not tell your kids the particulars about the divorce. You don't have to eat that later either. So perfect your elevator speech and stick with it. And think carefully before cutting someone out of the extended family, because it is very difficult to let an extruded OP back into the family circle.

We've emphasized the larger family unit as something immutable—divorced moms and dads will never not be a family. The OP and I split custody, photos, and anecdotes. Before you roll your eyes, let me assure you we are far from perfect. There are times when we are together and inside of ten seconds remember vividly why we never want to live together again. But I know there is one person on this planet who loves those kids as much as I do, and if I want to know what's going on and see photos and hear stories and experience more than 50 percent of their lives, I had better get the dignity thing together and be nice. We try to arrange our lives for optimal unity. We co-host birthdays. We celebrate holidays together. We communicate, we encourage the children to stay in touch with the OP, and we conspire together for surprises. I still don't want to live with him.

Some people feel we are sending our children mixed messages, giving them false hope. Not at all. They know in no uncertain terms that we will never be married again and will never live together again. They have seen and heard what other kids go through when their parents divorce. I've heard more than once about a friend who only sees mom once a year, or a dad who moved out of state, or parents who never speak—or speak ill of one another. That's when our children thank us. They know it could be much worse.

36 Fight Fair and Keep It Civil

Set words that are off-limits and respect them.

I know I said earlier that there is no such thing as "fair," but I'll use the term because everyone has a personal sense of what's fair. Suspend disbelief and stay with me.

Fighting fair is something that parents, teachers, clergy, rabbis, babysitters, siblings, and peers have hammered into your brain all your life. And yet fighting fair is extremely hard when emotions run high. Fair doesn't mean the same to everyone. Besides, there is a fine line between love and hate, and once it's crossed, fair is almost non-existent.

Since the definition of "fair" is mushy at best, you need to set certain ground rules for disagreements. Set words that are off-limits and respect them.

"Safe words" are words you can say to signal that all conversation needs to stop immediately because it is no longer possible for you to fight fair. Here are mine: "I need to stop right now, because I can no longer be civil. I'll come back and continue, but for now I need to retreat and regroup."

Notice I said "retreat." Retreat is not surrender. It is a protective and practical way to walk away, calm down, and rethink the issue. Words that are off-limits, on the other hand, are always off-limits.

If possible, work out how to react to words that are off-limits before things get heated. Be sure you both know and understand these words. Practice how you will exit a conversation that has gone off the road. Stash in your head ways to keep the wheels from coming off the car. Prepare a mental breakdown lane, to extend a tired metaphor.

Rehearse what you want to say. Be sure it is something you are willing for your neighbors, your children, your parents, or strangers to hear and judge you by. This is easier said than done, but it's preferable to having an uncomfortable conversation with your children. Here's one I had when one of my children ran out of the house and hid during an argument I was having with the OP.

> "I am sorry that your dad and I didn't handle ourselves well this morning; I am sorry we argued. But even if we were madly in love and still married, we would still argue. I know you've heard your friends' parents argue, so you can't go on blaming every little upset on the divorce."

> "I know."

> "You can't change your father. You can't control him. You can only control how you react. You can't control me, or change me. I am sorry that I am not the best mom I can be sometimes, but all you can do when it's bad is control your reaction. Our behavior was unacceptable and yours was unacceptable, so we all need to agree to start fresh with respect.

> "I love you and your siblings endlessly, but I am not here to make you happy. Happiness is a state, not a goal, and not a right. You are lucky when you are happy. I want you instead to be strong, to be able to handle disappointment, to argue constructively, and to look at things from all angles. I want you to know how to handle yourself, and understand how to let us handle ourselves. Dad and I will argue. Period. Today was not a fair fight. It made us all unhappy, but I will try to be better. I promise I will never intentionally hurt you. We can't control anything other than our own actions, but we'll learn together how to do that with dignity and grace. Okay?"

It sounds so wise, but it is so hard to practice when all you can hear is the sound of the other grownup calling you insane. There's a good example of a word that is off-limits.

37

Remember: Children Sense All, See a Lot and Hear More Than You May Think

Your children may not always remember what was said, but they will always remember how they felt when they heard it.

Your children see and hear far more than you can ever imagine. They talk about it together. They will also talk to others if they don't feel they can talk with you. If you are angry, bitter, and resentful, they are not going to feel safe opening up to you, and they are probably right.

Don't scare your children by wallowing in a funk. You can't sit out a depression without making your children sit it out with you. If you need help, get it. If they need help, give it. You don't get martyr points, but you do get points for making progress.

Progress may include sucking it up and being civil and cooperative with the OP's new partner. Do it even if it kills you a little inside. Your children will see it, appreciate it, and even relax a little knowing that you are able to put aside your differences so that they can have some semblance of a normal childhood.

Let your children know that if there is one place in the world where they're safe, it's with you. You are each other's home—even if you don't live in the same house anymore. You have a home so long as you are together. Recognize it, cherish it, and nurture it. The home that is you and your children will be grown up all too soon.

This is about creating safe spaces for them, not about making others miserable while you are miserable or protecting your turf as a parent. Think about this: you do NOT want your children to feel they have to apologize for your behavior to the new person in the OP's life. If you are trying to keep them from getting too close to that person, being rude, unkind, or hostile will only backfire and create sympathy in your children for the new partner. Take the high road. The view is always better.

Grow satisfied with your new life rather than waste time comparing your life to the OP's life. In one way or another, you each helped craft the circumstances leading up to divorce, and you must each do more work to craft new and better circumstances. Even if you feel that most of the fault lies with the other person, stifle it. Your children do not want to hear it. Work to create your new and better reality while letting as little of those feelings as possible thwart your creation. You really don't want to look around one day and realize you've replicated some part of your former misery and inflicted misery on your children.

Resentment takes up space in your brain and in your heart. It hangs hugely on your back and doesn't look good on you. Want your happy life and autonomy back? Make good choices before choices are forced on you. Pick a new direction, adjust your expectations, and go for it. If you wait for someone to hand you a fair deal, or a workable plan, you will wait a long, long time. And chances are that if you are waiting for someone else to define your future, you won't be satisfied with it. You weren't satisfied with what the OP offered you during marriage, so why should now be any different?

If you remember nothing else about this rule, remember this: your children may not always remember what was said, but they will always remember how they felt when they heard it.

Rule

38 Make a New Template for Relationships

You now have the chance to pursue a relationship with wisdom you didn't have back then, and a duty to pass that wisdom on to your children.

Children mimic what they see; promise yourself that someday you will show your children a mature, responsible, loving, and committed relationship.

The goal is to raise healthy, happy, well-adjusted children, so start by giving them a good example. If you and your OP were unable to show them what a loving, committed, dedicated team looked like, set out to find someone with whom you can. Children need to see their parents love and be loved, care and be cared for. They will imitate what they see, so try to let them catch you in the act of being kind and loving. These are the memories they will carry, and they will need five or six positive impressions to balance out each negative impression. You've got a lot of work to do, so choose well. It's a long life.

If they are like I was, never having witnessed a healthy parental relationship in my younger years, they will make bad choices until they make good ones. See if you can short-circuit that by showing them by example how not to sell yourself short. The fact that you are trying to make a better home and better life for yourself and your children speaks volumes about your character. Dating now is not the same as dating back then—character means so much more than a hot bod and perfect hair. (Thank God.)

I don't mean to make this sound easy—it's not—but I do want you to know that it will get better. It will get worse, then better, then worse again, and then REALLY better. There will be flashbacks but also flash-forwards in which you see a life you can love and be proud of. This is a good start toward taking inventory of the things you have and how much better they are than what you had while married.

Here's perspective for you: your marriage to the OP is the only subjective frame of reference your children have for what marriage is. In most cases, they've never seen their parents in another relationship. They will be at a total loss for how to process how in blue blazes anything good could ever come of dissolving the one union they've known.

You will need to let them mourn. You'll mourn with them (even if you're still seething, you will eventually remember SOMETHING fondly). It might take years, or maybe a lifetime. But, just as the OP will always be a part of their lives if you both want to remain parents, the fact will always remain that your dissolved marriage is the only one they've ever experienced. It's up to you to help them see relationships in a new light, and slowly prepare them for the realization that some things fail so that others can thrive. You now have the chance to pursue a relationship with wisdom you didn't have back then, and a duty to pass that wisdom on to your children.

Special note for parents of girls:

If your daughter does not carry a frame of reference for how a man should respect and love a woman, she will jump at the first boy who shows her the least bit of interest. She will sell herself short. Teach her how to value herself!

Special note for parents of boys:

Someone wiser than I am once said, "If you want to know how your husband will treat you, look carefully at how he treats his mother." You're not only raising a boy to be a man, you are training him to be a good husband and father. Insist on respect and manners. Teach him to be a gentleman!

39 Your Life Will Be Better after Divorce, or at Least Acceptably Different

You can't get apples from a pear tree. I know. I spent years shaking that trunk and being mad at the tree.

Major life changes are stressful, even when they are for the better. Any sort of prolonged or extreme stress can upset the brain's chemical balance. If you feel you might benefit from counseling or medication (or yoga or exercise for that matter), GET IT.

Have you noticed that folks never seem to hesitate to recommend exercise, which is just about the last thing most depressed people feel like doing? People who haven't been there may not understand that at all. Not that I'm speaking from experience or anything (NO, I DO NOT WANT TO GO FOR A RUN; I WANT ICE CREAM!).

Treat your mental health with the same level of respect you would give your physical health. It may be impossible to imagine that anything could make you feel better right now. Personally, I'm still upright and sane today because of Big Pharma. Getting my anxiety and anger under control kept me from sobbing all day, and treating my depression kept me functioning when my children (and I) needed me most.

Getting help evened out my mental landscape, filling in potholes and shaving off jagged edges. It softened the highs, but it also took away the lows that were keeping me from functioning normally. I felt like myself again and was able to practice tolerance while letting go of hostility and anger. Things that would have sent me into an apoplectic fit didn't anymore. Insults and arguments slid off my shoulders, without taking my pride or dignity with them. I stopped being afraid of my own head. Serenity is highly underrated. OK, scratch serenity. Sanity is good enough most days.

A reader of my blog once emailed me describing her guilt over divorcing a man who had multiple affairs and spent a lot of their money on booze. She couldn't understand why he would choose alcohol and other women over her, and she was paralyzed over making a decision that was handicapped by her conviction that she was somehow the problem, and that she'd be compounding it by putting the children through a divorce. The following was my response to her:

> Life will be harder, much harder for a while, and you will feel awful for the children. That is the bad news. The good news is that it will never be as bad again as it was when you were with him, watching your life get worse. From now on, your life will get better.

> Seven years after divorce, I count all the ways my life is better: my kids have a mom (yeah, I was that depressed sometimes); they have a sane mom; they have a mom that provides and cares for them. Someday (currently, actually), they will see mom in a mutually respectful, loving, RESPONSIBLE relationship. You were not going to be able to show them that with their dad, because he will not change. You have to teach them that if things are bad and can only get better with change, then embrace change, or at least surrender to it.

I tell my kids we are a better team in two houses. I don't know if that will be the case with you, but think of it this way: you can both stay parents, but you don't have to live together. Once you are divorced you are no longer jointly responsible for any bad financial, social, domestic, or behavioral decisions he makes. I cannot emphasize that enough. You can write your own ticket and give those kids the example you think they should have, and minimize exposure to the ones they shouldn't have.

40 Take Periodic Inventory on Where You Are in the Grief Process

You may want to lock yourself in a bakery and not come out for a week. This is normal.

I wavered about how to discuss the grief process. I asked a few friends. Ultimately, I got more out of reading the definition than I did from listening to others "cheerlead" me through it. (Besides, after a while their voices begin to sound like Charlie Brown's teacher, am I right?) So! Definition! This one is from good ole Wikipedia, something to tack to your refrigerator so you see it every time you reach for that wine and cheesecake:

> The **Kübler-Ross model**, commonly known as **The Five Stages of Grief**, is a theory first introduced by Elisabeth Kübler-Ross (http://bit.ly/NwAa2H)[13] in her book *On Death and Dying*... not everyone who experiences a life-threatening or life-altering event feels all five of the responses nor will everyone who does experience them do so in any particular order. The theory is that the reactions to illness, death, and loss are as unique as the person experiencing them. Some people may *get stuck* in one stage.

Stay with me here; there isn't a whole lot of difference between mourning a death and mourning a divorce. In some ways, it's worse, because you don't get to bury the other person. Heh. Little joke.

---

13. en.wikipedia.org/wiki/K%C3%BCbler-Ross_model

The stages, popularly known by the acronym **DABDA**, include:

1. **Denial**—"I feel fine."; "This can't be happening, not to me."
   Denial is usually only a temporary defense for the individual... Denial is a defense mechanism and some people can become locked in this stage.
2. **Anger**—"Why me? It's not fair!"; "How can this happen to me?"; "Who is to blame?"
   Once in the second stage, the individual recognizes that denial cannot continue. Because of anger, the person is very difficult to care for due to misplaced feelings of rage and envy... People can be angry with themselves, or with others, and especially those who are close to them. It is important to remain detached and nonjudgmental when dealing with a person experiencing anger from grief.
3. **Bargaining**—"I'll do anything for a few more years."; "I will give my life savings if..."
   The third stage involves the hope that the individual can somehow postpone or delay... Psychologically, the individual is saying, "I understand... but if I could just do something to buy more time..."
4. **Depression**—"I'm so sad, why bother with anything?"; "I'm going to die soon so what's the point?"; "I miss my loved one, why go on?"
   During the fourth stage, ...[one] begins to understand the certainty... the individual may become silent, refuse visitors and spend much of the time crying and grieving... It is not recommended to attempt to cheer up an individual who is in this stage. It is an important time for grieving that must be processed... Feeling those emotions shows that the person has begun to accept the situation.
5. **Acceptance**—"It's going to be okay."; "I can't fight it, I may as well prepare for it."In this last stage, individuals begin to come to terms.

In short, you will grieve. It will not be fun. You will want to punch things. You may want to lock yourself in a bakery and not come out for a week. This is normal.

Remember, pummeling someone is not a productive way to get some of that grief out. I much prefer Angry Playlists. Don't laugh. There are several in this household, loosely divided into categories such as Things Are So Much Better Now, You Idiot, I've Learned Oh So Much About Myself No Thanks To You, and just plain Angry. They all sound wonderful at top volume with the car windows down, barreling down a highway (at the legal speed limit, of course, with hands at ten and two on the steering wheel).

41

Keep Hope Alive for Future (Healthier) Relationships

Children hate divorce but often appreciate all the wonderful people who have come into their lives as a result.

I decided to include this rule just after marrying again in March 2012. It was the unlikeliest of scenarios for me. I thought there was no going back, ever, to that state of mind that fostered hope for the future, and—hand to God—hope for a lasting, loving, mutually awesome partnership with someone I loved and respected. A man who loved, respected, and knew me to my core. I used to think those were mutually exclusive qualities, at least in anyone who showed interest in me, but I discovered that—lo and behold—there actually are people out there who can and will make your life half as hard and twice as good.

I got lucky. I found love after divorce, a love worthy of a new marriage, on new terms.

And then I wrote my guy a letter that set forth all the things that I believed were possible so long as we protected our partnership and showed our six children that one could divorce and remarry and be better for it. I wanted to give them something we could never have given to them in our previous, unhappy marriages:

> I want us to be role models for them. I want our children to see how a man and a woman in love can go through the daily rituals in peace, without anger, without animosity, without beating each other up or scrabbling for dominance through belittling or condescension. I want them to see you tuck me in on the couch and bring me coffee, and I want them to see me snuggle up to you and scratch your head and listen to you talk about your day. I want them to see us both diving in and taking care of things-cooking,

laundry, responding to their needs, tending to sick ones, checking in constantly to be sure we all know where we are in the great scheme of things.

I want them to learn responsibility and understand how to earn things: respect, love, money, and status. It will be our challenge to set things up in a recognizable, consistent way so that there are clear relationships between effort and output. I want them to learn the difference between effort and garbage, and effort and gold. One is tolerable if the other is constantly being worked toward.

I don't want them to feel entitled. One thing our situation has done is to teach my children that life is not fair, that being a good person doesn't earn you good things, and that you have to make your own luck and be poised to take advantage of opportunities as they arise. It's why I spend so much time touching my children and using endearments and always welcoming their thoughts and feelings. You are the first man I have ever met that does that consistently and to a level that inspires me to do better.

We understand that about each other, and can tolerate imperfection, hell, embrace it, because life is messy and you can't recognize success until you've royally fucked things up. And it's OK to do that on a daily basis. Above all, I want them to see that laughter and closeness and tolerance and concern for others more than makes up for any discomfort that comes from failure or conflict. Get it in the open, understand it, have a laugh, get some ice cream. And then get up and do it all over again.

Whenever my kids reminisce about the days before our divorce, I remind them that if no one ever divorced, they would not have their stepbrothers. They would have one uncle instead of six uncles and an aunt, PLUS spouses and all the cousins that followed.

The bottom line is children hate divorce, but—at least in our family—they would never give up all the wonderful people who have come into our lives as a result.

42 These Are My Rules. What Are Yours?

*Let all of us
benefit from
your wisdom
(or take a
lesson from
your mistakes)!*

There is small chance that your divorce experience and mine will have everything in common; all divorces are different, difficult, and painful.

Predicting how a divorce will go is like predicting anything about home remodeling: chances are that it will take twice as long and cost three times as much. I'm guessing that the Founding Fathers wondered sometimes if they were starting a new way of life or remodeling an old one. For sure, both sides dragged it out and made some bad decisions, but in the end, peace came once both sides had a deal they could honor, one that left them dignity, and one that was sustainable. No one wants to have to be perpetually prepared for war.

Think of this as the re-founding of a family. It will be messy, inconvenient, and loud. There will be "creative differences." There will be budgetary and political conflicts. It will feel bloody and savage at times, but it will also open up new avenues of existence that simply weren't available when you were unhappily married.

Now that we're at the end, in Rule 42, I feel the need for a final huddle to make sure we've hit the high points again—it's important that plays are memorized and that you're ready to stay sharp and look to teammates when you can't advance on your own.

Here are the highlights—they may not be popular, but with hindsight, I hope they will seem wise:

- **Keep to the high ground!** The moment you stoop to match or outdo the OP's bad behavior, you've lost the advantage.
- **Always keep the kids' views in mind!** Consider how your actions will look and feel to the children. Will they be demoralized or damaged? Will they lose respect? If the answer is yes to either question, then don't do it! (Or at least have the grace to do it out of earshot.)
- **Clarity and details matter, and they are priceless in writing.** Once you've reached any kind of agreement, get it in writing so that any disagreement has an objective starting point for both of you (or for a mediator if that doesn't work).
- **Take care of yourself at least as much as you take care of your children!** If you are run-down and reduced to a husk of a person, they aren't getting any more out of you than you are.
- **You will be a better team in two households!** That means you have to work TOGETHER to make it possible for the children to heal and thrive. You can't wish each other away, so you may as well sack up, hold your nose, and make it work.
- **Always look forward, and ask for help when you need it!** You can argue all day long about fault and root cause, but what you, the OP, and your children need now is something to hope for and something to look forward to that is better than what came before.

Each of these rules should help you take inventory of where you are, what you have to work with, and how much better your life will be now that you are taking decisive action to create a better team in two households.

I predict that you will come out of this reading with a long list of your own rules, including some that I didn't include here. Promise me this: if you do, please share them!! Drop me a line, or even better, leave comments on the 42Rules.com web site where this book is sold. Let all of us benefit from your wisdom (or take a lesson from your mistakes)!

In the end, all we can do is try to do what is best for the kids, and for ourselves. Best of luck to you—I know you'll find your way, and will discover that life changes that seem destructive can in time be a blessing.

Books for Kids Going through Divorce

Dinosaurs Divorce
by Brown and Brown

It's Not Your Fault, Koko Bear
by Lansky

A Smart Girl's Guide to Her Parents' Divorce: How to Land on your Feet When Your World Turns Upside Down
by Holyoke and Nash

The Divorce Helpbook for Kids
by Cynthia MacGregor

The Divorce Helpbook for Teens
by Cynthia MacGregor

Now What Do I Do?: A Guide to Help Teenagers with Their Parents' Separation or Divorce
by Cassella-Kapusinski

B Online Divorce Support Communities

Divorce 360.com: divorce360.com provides help, advice and community for people contemplating, going through or recovering from divorce and the issues around it-custody, child support, alimony and litigation. (http://divorce360.com)

Wikivorce: Wikivorce is a well-respected, award winning social enterprise, volunteer-run, government sponsored, and charity funded. It helps 50,000 people a year through divorce. (http://www.wikivorce.com/divorce/)

Divorce Advice for Women: Helping Women Survive Divorce and Rebuild Their Lives

Daily Strength: Free, anonymous support from people just like you.

Divorce Care: Divorce Care is a divorce recovery support group where you can find help and healing for the hurt of separation and divorce. (http://www.divorcecare.org/)

Child-Centered Divorce Network: A Support Network for Parents (http://www.childcentereddivorce.com)

Clarify You: Supporting You Through Change (http://www.clarifyyou.com)

Virginia Gilbert CFT: Specializing in High-Conflict Divorce, Challenging Children, Adoptions, and Partners of Sex Addicts (http://virginiagilbertmft.com/)

Divorcing Divas: It's not the end...it's the beginning (http://divorcingdivas.com/)

There are support groups specifically for men, women, or children experiencing the divorce process. Google is your friend. Use it wisely.

Family Scheduling Tools

A schedule is useless unless all parties agree to, are aware of, and follow it. Check out these babies:

Famjama (http://www.famjama.com/) is a free online family organizer that facilitates access by multiple family members. Maintain a custom group on the website famjama.com and choose to make the information Public/Private depending upon the need. Features and benefits include the following:

- Allows more than just recording family events
- Facilitate Mobile access to the online calendar
- Synchronize the online calendar to iPhone Ical
- Allow a user to update or add an event to another user's calendar within a group
- Enable E-mail, SMS or Facebook notifications of the updates to the schedules
- Export to different online calendar systems like Google Calendar
- Store important contacts
- Bulletin list of events and flagging of specific events on the calendar

Cozi (http://www.cozi.com) is a free online family organizer and includes organizer tools like family calendar for schedules, grocery-shopping lists and family to do lists and detailed family journals for making family notes. Since the organizer is a web-based application, you can access the application from anywhere in the world.

There is one central online calendar that can be color-coded for your family, and you can add events with descriptions. One account can be used by all family members, and it has push notifications so each member can be notified by email of upcoming items. Features and benefits include the following:

- Online shopping list
- To do lists
- Reminders and messages
- Family Journal
- Synchronizes with MS Outlook

Family Crossings (http://www.familycrossings.com/) is another free family website where you can set up family calendars, upload photo albums, create family task lists, and even have family chats.

This is not just a calendar, it's an organizer that can track extended family and act as a sort of "where are they now and what are they up to?" tracker. Features and benefits include the following:

- Create and share family calendars, family shopping lists, photos, tips, and news from wherever you reside
- Share stories and private email between family members
- Chat live with family around the globe
- Quickly send daily family schedules, family events, and the like to relations around the world
- Send Christmas and other holiday greetings only to family instantly
- Send family photos online quickly and safely
- Database and forum included
- Free version gives you 250MB of free space online, so you can upload your important photos, but it is not an unlimited photo sharing website

Our Family Wizard (http://www.ourfamilywizard.com) helps ensure that co-parenting and child custody issues are manageable. You can create parenting time schedules/plans in minutes, share activities, trade days, track child support, send messages, make journal entries, and keep accurate records in one convenient place.

It's not free, but last I looked, $200 is about what you'd pay for a single therapy session. I love that you can track expenses, tally up, and make payments back and forth right there. I also love that it lets you TRADE DAYS. I am seriously jumping up and down in my chair about this feature. It helps to have a written, shared record. I have recommended to more than one friend that they spring for this instead of a few rounds at the bar. Features and benefits include the following:

- Calendar that lets you create parenting plans and activities, trade days, and keep accurate records
- Journal for private or shared entries so you can document what really happened and create printable reports
- Expense Log
- Shared expense tracking with date and time stamps
- Approval process
- Info
- Safe storage and back-up
- Well organized sections that cover medical, school and more
- A Notification System for email or texts

If you are both Google users and willing to use shared calendars, **Google Calendar** (https://www.google.com/calendar/) may be all you need. Subscribe to each other's calendars, and/or create a shared one. It's one of the best tools on the web, and it's FREE.

D | Additional Information on Child Support

The following excerpts are taken directly from the *Department of Child Support Services Handbook*, downloadable as a PDF.

> Mission of the [CA] Department of Child Support Services
>
> > The mission of the Department of Child Support Services is to promote the well-being of children and the self-sufficiency of families by delivering effective child support services to help meet the financial, medical, and emotional needs of children.

There is great information on the following subjects in Section 1 of the *Handbook*, entitled "Services Offered by the Child Support Program":

- Establishing paternity (fatherhood)
- Locating parents
- Requesting child support orders from the court
- Requesting medical support orders
- Collecting and distributing child support

Ooh, this is good, from page 19 of the *Handbook*:

- Q: If I lose my job, do I still have to pay child support?
- A: Yes. But call the county Department of Child Support Services right away. Ask them to review your case. The court can modify the child support order if you lost your job through no fault of your own.

Another great article:

What Can Child Support Be Used For? (Posted on Law-yers.com)

Child Support Should Pay for Basic Needs

Technically, child support is supposed to cover housing, food, and clothing, but the costs of raising a child usually involve more than just these basic needs. There are expenses for school and after-school activities and for toys. Older teenagers might have car costs, such as auto insurance or gasoline.

Most child support payments easily cover a child's share of the household's basic expenses, with some money left over. A custodial parent can reasonably spend that money on the extras.

Custodial Parents Don't Have to Report on Spending

Because custodial parents don't have to submit an accounting to the court for their child support spending, it's possible that a parent could spend the money—or at least some of it—on the parent's personal needs. If a non-custodial parent suspects this is happening, he or she can notify the court, but probably won't get much of a response unless the child's needs are actually being ignored or neglected. Some states will order parents to mediation to try to work the problem out, but judges will rarely do much more than that.

Appendix

E Divorce Playlists

These are a few suggestions from my own and other people's cathartic "divorce" playlists. Yes, there are a number of songs from P!nk and quite a few country-western songs, but hey, the shoe fits. All I know is that I might have lost my mind completely if I hadn't spent a lot of time barreling down the highway, singing along to some of these songs that nail the angst and articulate things you'd LIKE to say, but WON'T, because you are practicing dignity and grace. RIGHT?

- "21 Guns" by Green Day
- "99 Problems" by Hugo
- "A Better Son/Daughter" by Rilo Kiley
- "According to You" by Orianthi
- "All I Ever Do" by Lori McKenna
- "Anyone Else" by The Mouldy Peaches
- "Been a Long Day" by Rosi Golan
- "Better Than I Used to Be" by Tim McGraw
- "Breakeven (Falling to Pieces)" by The Script
- "Can't Cry Anymore" by Sheryl Crow
- "Chasing Cars" by Snow Patrol
- "Coming Home" by Diddy - Dirty Money & Skylar Grey
- "Different Kinds of Happy" by Sara Groves
- "Divorce Song" by Liz Phair (my personal favorite)
- "F**kin Perfect" by P!nk
- "Funhouse" by P!nk
- "Giving It Up for You" by Holly Brook
- "Good Riddance (Time of Your Life)" by Green Day
- "Grace" by Saving Jane
- "Guitars, Cadillacs" by Dwight Yoakam
- "Gunpowder & Lead" by Miranda Lambert

- "Hell No" by Sondra Lerche
- "Hemingway's Whiskey" by Kenny Chesney
- "Hopelessly Stoned" by Hugo
- "I Don't Believe You" by P!nk
- "I'll Be OK" by Sondra Lerche
- "I'm Movin' On" by Rascal Flatts
- "If Love is a Red Dress" by Maria McKee
- "Impossible" by Shontelle
- "In the Air Tonight" by Phil Collins
- "It's All Your Fault" by P!nk
- "It's Going to Be Alright" by Sara Groves
- "Like a Fool" by Shelby Lynne
- "Like Me" by Chely Wright
- "Little Broken Hearts" by Norah Jones
- "Mean" by P!nk
- "Misery" by The BoDeans
- "Misfit" by Amy Studt
- "My Hands are Shaking" by Sondra Lerche
- "Need You Now" by Lady Antebellum
- "No Woman No Cry" by Bob Marley
- "Not a Pretty Girl" by Ani DiFranco
- "Nothing Compares 2 U" by Sinead O'Connor
- "Now I'm That Bitch" by Livvi Franc
- "One Thing" by Finger Eleven
- "Please Call Me, Baby" by Tom Waits
- "Please Don't Leave Me" by P!nk
- "Pray for You" by Jaron and the Long Road to Love
- "Record Lady" by Lyle Lovett
- "Right Where I Need to Be" by Gary Allan
- "Save Me" by Aimee Mann
- "Set Fire to the Rain" by Adele
- "She Hates Me" by Puddle of Mudd
- "She's 22" by Norah Jones
- "Shut Up and Drive" by Chely Wright
- "Sin for a Sin" by Miranda Lambert
- "Smoke Rings In the Dark" by Gary Allan
- "So What" by P!nk
- "Sober" by P!nk
- "Songs About Rain" by Gary Allan
- "Stay" by Sugarland
- "Sunday Mornin' Comin' Down" by Kris Kristofferson
- "That's How You Know" by Lori McKenna
- "The Blower's Daughter" by Damien Rice
- "The Cowboy in Me" by Tim McGraw
- "The Last Day of Our Acquaintance" by Sinead O'Connor
- "The Toll" by Black Rebel Motorcycle Club

- "Three Little Birds" by Bob Marley
- "Twice as Good" by Sara Groves
- "U + Ur Hand" by P!nk
- "Undo It" by Carrie Underwood
- "Unstoppable" by Rascal Flatts
- "Watching Airplanes" by Gary Allan
- "Whiskey Lullaby" by Alison Krauss & Brad Paisley
- "Why Did I Ever Like You" by P!nk
- "Wreck You" by Heidi Newfield
- "You're Not Sorry" by Taylor Swift

More Divorce Quotes

Daily I walk around my small, picturesque town with a thought bubble over my head: Person Going Through A Divorce. When I look at other people, I automatically form thought bubbles over their heads. Happy Couple With Stroller. Innocent Teenage Girl With Her Whole Life Ahead Of Her. Content Grandmother And Grandfather Visiting Town Where Their Grandchildren Live With Intact Parents. Secure Housewife With Big Diamond. Undamaged Group Of Young Men On Skateboards. Good Man With Baby In Baby Björn Who Loves His Wife. Dogs Who Never Have To Worry. Young Kids Kissing Publicly. Then every so often I see one like me, one of the shambling gaunt women without makeup, looking older than she is: Divorcing Woman Wondering How The Fuck This Happened.
—Suzanne Finnamore, *Split: A Memoir of Divorce*

The difference between a divorce and a legal separation is that a legal separation gives a husband time to hide his money.
—Johnny Carson quotes (American TV Host, 1925-2005)

There is no such thing as a "broken family." Family is family, and is not determined by marriage certificates, divorce papers, and adoption documents. Families are made in the heart. The only time family becomes null is when those ties in the heart are cut. If you cut those ties, those people are not your family. If you make those ties, those people are your family.

And if you hate those ties, those people will still be your family because whatever you hate will always be with you.
—C. JoyBell C.

A divorce is like an amputation; you survive, but there's less of you.
—Margaret Atwood, Time Magazine, Mar. 19, 1973

I've been through divorce and will always be a "divorced kid"... For me, my parent's divorce was hard at first, but I overcame my sadness and my fears about it. I know that my parents are happier apart. And I'm happy with the way things are, too... Divorce can sometimes be for the better. You may end up with happier parents, and you will definitely learn a lot about yourself! And that's the whole point of growing up. So if you think about it, there are reasons to be happy about this experience, if you can learn and grow from it.
—Zoe Stern, Divorce Is Not the End of the World

You know, that's the only good thing about divorce; you get to sleep with your mother.
—Clare Booth Luce, The Women

But in the real world, you couldn't really just split a family down the middle, mom on one side, dad the other, with the child equally divided between. It was like when you ripped a piece of paper into two: no matter how you tried, the seams never fit exactly right again. It was what you couldn't see, those tiniest of pieces that were lost in the severing, and their absence kept everything from being complete.
—Sarah Dessen, What Happened to Goodbye

Divorce is the psychological equivalent of a triple coronary by-pass. After such a monumental assault on the heart, it takes years to amend all the habits and attitudes that led up to it.
—Mary Kay Blakely

The less said, the better.
—Unknown

Divorce is a declaration of independence with only two signers.
—Gerard Lieberman

Learn from the mistakes of others. You can't live long enough to make them all yourself.
—Unknown

There is a rhythm to the ending of a marriage just like the rhythm of a courtship—only backward. You try to start again but get into blaming over and over. Finally you are both worn out, exhausted, hopeless. Then lawyers are called in to pick clean the corpses. The death has occurred much earlier.
—Erica Jong, How To Save Your Own Life

"Bad divorce?" Hardy asked, his gaze falling to my hands. I realized I was clutching my purse in a death grip.

"No, the divorce was great," I said. "It was the marriage that sucked."
—Lisa Kleypas, Blue-Eyed Devil

A divorce lawyer is a chameleon with a law book.
—Marvin Mitchelson

Ah, yes, divorce... from the Latin word meaning to rip out a man's genitals through his wallet.
—Robin Williams

Marriage is grand. Divorce is about twenty grand.
—Jay Leno, The Tonight Show

Divorce is the one human tragedy that reduces everything to cash.
—Anonymous

Getting married in America is like doing business in Russia. Everything is up for grabs, everything is constantly renegotiated, and nobody has to keep [his or her] word. I think that makes for a lot of unhappy marriages, even though no-fault was supposed to take care of that.
—John Crouch, interview on the "Time Out" show with Jim Parmelee

I know God will not give me anything I can't handle. I just wish that He didn't trust me so much.
—Mother Theresa

There cannot be a crisis today; my schedule is already full.
—Unknown

You will either step forward into growth or you will step back into safety.
—Abraham Maslow

Courage is being afraid but going on anyhow.
—Dan Rather

The only thing more unthinkable than leaving was staying; the only thing more impossible than staying was leaving. I didn't want to destroy anything or anybody. I just wanted to slip quietly out the back door, without causing any fuss or consequences, and then not stop running until I reached Greenland.
—Elizabeth Gilbert, *Eat, Pray, Love*

I don't miss him, I miss who I thought he was.
—Unknown

What I wanted on the other side of all this pain wasn't to win, to be right, or even just to be able to claim the cruddy consolation prize of being the one who was wronged. What I wanted was peace.
—Stacey Morrison, Falling Apart in One Piece

They may already know too much about their mother and father—nothing being more factual than divorce, where so much has to be explained and worked through intelligently (though they have tried to stay equable). I've noticed this is often the time when children begin calling their parents by their first names, becoming little ironists after their parents' faults. What could be lonelier for a parent than to be criticized by his child on a first-name basis?
—Richard Ford, The Sportswriter

Show me a person who has never made a mistake and I'll show you somebody who has never achieved much.
—Joan Collins

For a couple with young children, divorce seldom comes as a "solution" to stress, only as a way to end one form of pain and accept another.
—Fred Rogers, Mister Rogers Talks With Parents

When two divorced people marry, four people get into bed.
—Jewish Proverb

For some reason, we see divorce as a signal of failure, despite the fact that each of us has a right, and an obligation, to rectify any other mistake we make in life.
—Joyce Brothers

About the Author

http://themommyblog.com
http://melindaroberts.net

Melinda Roberts is a pioneer in the blogging community, founding The Mommy Blog in 2002. Witty, sarcastic, and engaging, her writing has been described as a cross between Erma Bombeck, Nora Ephron, and Helen Fielding. Melinda has appeared on Oprah, CNN, ABC, Fox, CBS and other fancy media outlets. Her first book, Mommy Confidential: Adventures from the Wonderbelly of Motherhood was nominated for The Blooker Prize in 2006.

Newly remarried, Melinda and her husband live with their six children in the Bay Area.

You can find her online at:
http://themommyblog.com and
http://melindaroberts.net.

42 Rules Program

A lot of people would like to write a book, but only a few actually do. Finding a publisher, and distributing and marketing the book are challenges that prevent even the most ambitious authors from getting started.

If you want to be a successful author, we'll provide you the tools to help make it happen. Start today by completing a book proposal at our website http://42rules.com/write/.

For more information, email info@superstarpress.com or call 408-257-3000.

Other Happy About Books

42 Rules for Working Moms

This book is a compilation of sensible advice from professional moms condensed into an easy-to-pick up, hard-to-put-down paperback format.

Paperback: $19.95
eBook: $14.95

Care: You Have the Power!

The intended audience includes parents, educators, anyone in social services or the medical field, managers and employees in business or non-profit organizations.

Paperback: $19.95
eBook: $14.95

42 Rules for Divorcing with Children

42 Rules for Sensible Investing

Leon Shirman shares his practical insights on personal investment strategies and philosophies, and on picking winning stocks.

Paperback: $19.95
eBook: $14.95

30 Day BootCamp: Your Ultimate Life Makeover

A step-by-step program that will teach you all of the tips, tricks, and techniques you need to get back in the driver's seat of your life.

Paperback: $19.95
eBook: $14.95

Purchase these books at Happy About
http://happyabout.com/
or at other online and physical bookstores.

A Message From Super Star Press™

Thank you for your purchase of this 42 Rules Series book. It is available online at:
http://happyabout.com/42rules/divorcingwithchildren.php or at other online and physical bookstores. To learn more about contributing to books in the 42 Rules series, check out
http://superstarpress.com.

Please contact us for quantity discounts at
sales@superstarpress.com.

If you want to be informed by email of upcoming books, please email
bookupdate@superstarpress.com.

Made in the USA
Middletown, DE
04 February 2016